THE DAILY DISASTER

REAL-LIFE STORIES OF 30 AMAZING DISASTERS

BY CORMAC O'BRIEN AND THE STAFF OF *THE DAILY DISASTER*

THE DAILY DISASTER

ESTABLISHED 1850

EDITOR-IN-CHIEF
Cormac O'Brien

STAFF SCIENTISTS
Professor Cornelius · Professor Cornelius, Jr ·
Professor Cornelius III · Professor Cornelius IV

STAFF PHYSICISTS
M. C. Squared · M. V. Squared · Moe Mentum

STAFF ECOLOGISTS
Forrest Greenacre · Autumn Greenacre · Rose Greenacre

STAFF GEOLOGISTS
Clay Marblerock · Shale Marblerock

STAFF METEOROLOGISTS
Hugh Midditee · Harry Kane · Wayne DeLay · Harry Kane, Jr.

STAFF TRAVEL CORRESPONDENTS
Anita Holliday · Ben Daire

STAFF LINGUIST
Frank O'File

STAFF SAFETY CONSULTANTS
Sergeant Safety · Captain Caution

MANAGING EDITORS
Erin Slonaker · Paige Araujo

DESIGN DIRECTOR
Jacqueline Spadaro

ART DIRECTOR
Bryn Ashburn

PHOTO EDITOR
Susan Oyama

ILLUSTRATORS
Bryn Ashburn · Christine Sheller

COPY EDITOR
Eileen Favorite

Copyright © 2002 by Quirk Productions, Inc.

A Quirk Book
www.quirkproductions.com

Scholastic and Tangerine Press and associated logos are trademarks of Scholastic Inc

Published by Tangerine Press, an imprint of Scholastic Inc; 557 Broadway;
New York, NY 10012

10 9 8 7 6 5 4 3 2 1

ISBN 0-439-38473-7

Printed and bound in Singapore

THE DAILY DISASTER

INTRODUCTION

BRACE YOURSELF FOR A DISASTER!

Imagine you're at home watching television. The couch is comfortable, your chocolate milk is tasty, and your favorite cartoon is making you wish you never had to go to school again. Suddenly, the chocolate milk starts to quiver in its glass. You feel movement beneath you, as if something in the couch is trembling. What's going on? Then it gets worse: You hear the windows rattle, and your mother's silly little statues start to jump and hop across the mantel. It hits you: earthquake! By the time you've figured out what's happening, everything is shaking, plates are crashing, wood is creaking, and dust is falling from the ceiling. Better find a safe place to hide...

Now picture yourself walking to your friend's house one afternoon. It's been overcast all day, but now it looks even worse. The clouds are heavy and gray. Knowing it's about to rain, you quicken your steps, eager to get to your friend's place before you get soaked. But what's that sound you begin to hear? It's a deep roar, almost like an approaching freight train. You look around, confused, and spot it: tornado! It moves slowly along the horizon, a black, twisting funnel, throwing up huge clouds of dirt. Then you watch as it rips into a barn, sending walls flying like paper and sucking the roof up into a violent sky. Now you're sprinting to your friend's place...

Disasters—like earthquakes and tornadoes—are awesome, terrifying, and often deadly. But wherever and whenever they occur, you can be sure we're there to report it. We're the staff of *The Daily Disaster*, and stuff like this is what we're all about. For over a hundred years, we've covered tragedies around the world, from volcanoes in the Caribbean to floods in Pakistan. This book features thirty of our best stories. You'll read about raging hurricanes, sinking ships, exploding zeppelins, even floods of molasses (that's right, molasses).

We hope you'll find these stories as exciting, fascinating, and downright scary as we have. But we also hope you take something with you, too—our staff scientists provide insider knowledge into the forces that caused the disaster, with experiments and simulations you can do at home. We also hope you'll learn what disasters teach us: that, no matter how much we think we know about science, nature will always be able to catch us by surprise. With the knowledge you'll gain from reading our best issues, you're sure to be prepared!

PHOTO CREDITS

THE DAILY DISASTER

Tuesday, October 10, 1871   Volume XXI No. 283   Price: 1 cent

BLAZING INFERNO COOKS CHICAGO TO A CRISP

Cow blamed for starting fire

CHICAGO, ILLINOIS—After two terrible days of raging fire, Chicago has been barbecued as thoroughly as any of the beefsteaks for which the great cattle town is famous. As many as 300 souls are feared to have perished.

The fire started shortly after 9:00 P.M. this past Sunday on the city's West Side. By 1:30 the following morning, the flames had jumped the Chicago River's south branch and set the business district ablaze, claiming the courthouse and the new "fireproof" offices of the *Chicago Tribune*. Driven by a steady wind from the southwest, the blaze continued northward across the main river. Sometime around 3:00 A.M., the roof collapsed over the water-pumping station, destroying any hope of stopping the inferno's progress.

(continued on page 2)

Hundreds of people race across the river to escape the burning city of Chicago.

CUD-CHEWING PERPETRATOR?

It is reliably reported that the fire began in the crowded barn of the O'Leary homestead on DeKoven Street, where, according to Mrs. O'Leary herself, no fewer than five cows were in residence. It seems possible that one of the careless bovines inadvertently kicked over a lantern, setting the barn's store of hay ablaze. It is not presently known whether the cows survived the conflagration.

The Daily Disaster would like to take this opportunity to remind our readers NOT to place dangerous items (lanterns, torches, or firearms) near cows, a clumsy species of animal. We're counting on you to keep our farmhouses safe.

IN OTHER NEWS

FIRES ALSO IN WISCONSIN

A fire has started naturally in the forests of Wisconsin. Turn to NATIONAL NEWS

"THE GREATEST SHOW ON EARTH"

Citizens of Brooklyn, New York, flock to see Mr. P. T. Barnum's amazing circus. Turn to ENTERTAINMENT.

DR. LIVINGSTONE, I PRESUME?

Journalist Sir Henry Stanley still searching for Dr. David Livingstone in Africa. Turn to CURRENT AFFAIRS.

FIRE SURVIVAL TIP
With Sergeant Safety

Catching fire can be terrifying, but whatever you do, don't run. The fire will just keep running with you. Remember:

Drop: Lie on the ground as quickly as you can.

Roll: Cover your face (especially your eyes) with your hands and roll over and over, back and forth. This will extinguish the flames by depriving them of the air they need to burn.

Go ahead and try it right now (it's kind of fun, actually). Pretend your clothes are on fire. Remember to make sure you roll back and forth enough to put out those flames—your life depends on it!

(continued from page 1)
By midday Monday, it had reached the northern edge of the city on Fullerton Avenue. "Mercifully, a steady rain saved us this morning," said 45-year-old resident Mitsy Malone. "It rescued us from the disaster we ourselves seemed powerless to stop."

The damage is severe: officials believe some 18,000 buildings were consumed, incurring an estimated $200,000 in damages. Perhaps as many as 100,000 citizens of this stricken metropolis, once called the Garden City of the West, are now homeless. In all, some 200 acres of the city's heart have been scorched, and rescue efforts are still impossible in many places—the ruins are simply too hot to enter. Pillars of smoke and steam can be seen everywhere, presenting a terrible vision of desolation and ruin. Adding to the city's plight are countless hoodlums who have come from all over the countryside in search of easy loot.

"I'm not surprised at all by any of this," states 30-year-old Chicagoan Meg Kunster. "The summer was exceptionally hot and dry in these parts, and small, localized fires have been a regular occurrence." Twenty were recorded the previous week alone. So common

EYEWITNESSES SPEAK:

Jacob Guntherson, 35, bank teller:
"Well, it's a terrible thing when your fellow man takes advantage of you in times of distress. I saw plenty of folks coming round with wagons, offering to cart people and valuables to safety, but only for a price. Thievery, I say, just plain thievery."

Roger Ascot, 57, civil servant:
"I am proud to say that I was with the right honorable Mayor Roswell B. Mason, yessir, with him throughout that terrible Sunday night. He arrived at the courthouse around midnight, full o' vim and vigor, sendin' out telegrams, issuing orders, following the progress of the conflagration. Once the courthouse caught fire, why, we all had to beg him to leave lest the flames send him to Eternity."

Martin "Swifty" McAlistar, 34, scoundrel and ne'er-do-well:
"I was in that goshdarn courthouse Monday mornin' with the other prisoners when it started blazin'. Then some fella came chargin' in, just in the lick o' time, and unlocked our cells. It's a good thing, too, 'cause the bell in the tower came a-crashin' down on the very place where we was waitin' just a moment before."

were they, in fact, that many citizens responded to rumors of fire on Sunday night with nothing more than weary annoyance, helping to prevent the sense of urgency that might have stopped this disaster before it raged out of control.

Adding to the tragedy were faulty fire alarm boxes. Connected to the courthouse by telegraph wire, they are designed for local residents to alert authorities as soon as any flames are seen. Unfortunately, the alarm box nearest to the origin of Sunday's blaze, on DeKoven Street, is believed to have malfunctioned.

THE DAILY DISASTER

Saturday, June 1, 1889 | Volume XXXIX No. 152 | Price: 1 cent

WALL OF WATER SMASHES JOHNSTOWN, PENNSYLVANIA

Dam gives way, unleashes lake onto victims

JOHNSTOWN, PENNSYLVANIA— It's not every day that an entire lake goes rampaging across the countryside. But that's precisely what Lake Conemaugh did yesterday afternoon when the dam that held it gave way. In the terrible flash flood that followed, the small Pennsylvania town east of Pittsburgh was virtually washed away, and more than 2,000 souls went with it.

Heavy rains have been coming down across the region for the past two days. By yesterday afternoon, Lake Conemaugh was dangerously high, threatening to spill over the South Fork Dam that contained it. The South Fork Fishing and Hunting Club, which owned the lake, was aware of the danger. They sent workers to dig an outlet off the lake, which would have relieved some of the pressure on the dam.

(continued on page 2)

Houses and businesses were destroyed in yesterday's terrible flood.

WEALTHY OWNERS OF LAKE TO BLAME?

Lake Conemaugh and the South Fork Dam were both owned by the South Fork Fishing and Hunting Club, whose 66 members included such millionaires as Andrew Carnegie and Henry Clay Frick. The dam was originally built in 1853 as part of the Pennsylvania canal system. The club bought the lake in 1879 and built a lodge on its banks as a base for their sporting activities. Although they spent plenty of money on the resort, they didn't spend much on the dam— which they attempted to modernize without the expertise of an engineer. Without proper upkeep, it's no wonder the dam finally fell apart, dooming thousands in the valley below.

IN OTHER NEWS

FRENCH ARCHITECT REACHES FOR THE SKY

Gaze upon images of Gustave Eiffel's tower, the tallest structure in the world, built in Paris for the World's Fair. See ENGINEERING FEATS.

A LEGENDARY READ

Read an excerpt from Mark Twain's latest story, *A Connecticut Yankee in King Arthur's Court*. See LITERATURE.

MOVING PICTURES

Thomas Edison works on building a new camera to take motion pictures, called the *kinetograph*. See ENTERTAINMENT.

(continued from page 1)

One of them was 18-year-old Anthony Fudrucker: "We labored frantically through the afternoon," he said, "but the rain fell faster than we could dig. We just started panicking when it looked like we were gonna lose the fight."

By 3:10 P.M. the South Fork Dam could withstand the enormous pressure no longer, and it gave way. Freed from its prison against the mountain, Lake Conemaugh crashed into the valley below with a deafening roar, emptying 20 million tons (18 million metric tons) of water in only 40 minutes. Half a mile wide and as tall as 75 feet (23 m), the wet wall of destruction raced along the Little Conemaugh River toward the 10,000 inhabitants of Johnstown. It made a few stops along the way. First was the little town of South Fork, two miles (3.2 km) away, where more than 20 homes were destroyed. Mineral Point, East Conemaugh, and Woodvale met similar fates.

By the time the huge wave struck Johnstown, almost an hour had passed since the dam had broken. "The flood was loaded with tons of debris—houses, barns, animals, wagons, trees," said 50-year-old survivor Lisa Phipps, "and it resembled a rolling mountain, so filthy was its water." Because all the telegraph lines were down, there was little warning. It broke upon the community with horrific force, demolishing buildings and sweeping away everything before it. In 10 minutes, it was all over. More disaster was to come. Downstream from Johnstown, an enormous pile of debris had collected against an old stone bridge that spans the Little Conemaugh. Last night it caught fire, burning the 80 survivors who had sought refuge there.

Four square miles (6.4 sq. km) of Johnstown have been completely destroyed. Over 1,500 homes have virtually vanished. Picking up the pieces will be long, hard work, but the town seems ready for the challenge.

HERO OF THE WEEK

After the torrent swept through Johnstown, Maxwell McAchren was holding on for dear life aboard a roof with a dozen other people, floating down the Little Conemaugh River. Suddenly, he spotted a six-year-old girl on a raft, screaming for help. The child was some distance away, but McAchren—despite the urgent pleas of his fellows not to do so—jumped into the water. He swam to the girl's raft, and climbed aboard.

After cruising for some time, he spotted a group of men on the shore, helping people out as they floated by. They called to McAchren to throw them the youngster, which he did—a full 15 feet (4.5 m) over the water into their waiting arms. It is not presently known what happened to this valiant young man; we can only hope that he is safe and sound.

ARE YOU A BLOCKHEAD?

With Professor Cornelius

Damming up water is no easy task, and this activity will show you why.

What You Need:

  A low tub or bucket (not the kind of bucket you take to the beach)

  Blocks or bricks (wooden blocks will work fine)

  Water

What You'll Do:

1. Take the blocks and build a wall across the center of the tub.

   Your wall won't be watertight, but that's OK—it's part of the experiment.

2. Slowly pour water into one side of the tub.

   You'll notice, of course, that some of the water leaks out into the other half.

3. Remove one of the blocks from the top of the wall.

   Watch the water go! The pressure of the water will be too much and it will break through the wall. Now you've seen what happens when a dam breaks in a river.

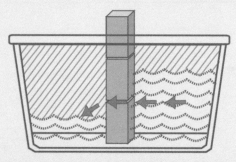

THE DAILY DISASTER

Tuesday, June 16, 1896 — Volume XLVI No. 168 — Price: 2 cents

TSUNAMI THRASHES JAPANESE COAST

Tens of thousands swept away by giant wave

IN OTHER NEWS

OUT TO SEA

Exactly one week ago, George Harbo and Frank Samuelson left New York in a tiny boat, bound for Europe. Will they survive to become the first men to row across the Atlantic Ocean? See PEOPLE AND PLACES.

CRIMINALS MAKE A BREAKTHROUGH OF THEIR OWN

Ever since the newfangled automobile started turning up in greater numbers, it was bound to happen—the first car theft occurred just a week ago. See SOCIETY.

BROTHER, CAN YOU SPARE A DIME?

The first "movie theater" is scheduled to open next week—but locals are already complaining about the ten cent ticket price. See ENTERTAINMENT.

SANRIKU, JAPAN—If you can imagine what a 100-foot (30-m) wall of water looks like, then you have some idea of the view recently from the shores of Japan. Without warning, a deadly tsunami (pronounced *soo-nah-mee*) struck the coast of the region of Sanriku yesterday evening, wiping out whole villages and killing an estimated 26,000 people. It is, without a doubt, the deadliest such disaster ever to have struck Japan.

Large crowds were gathered on the coast of Sanriku yesterday for the local holiday known as Boys' Festival. "It was a beautiful evening," recalled 29-year-old survivor Satoru Wakeshima, one of the few to miraculously endure the enormous wave. "Suddenly, I felt a very faint shock, like a vibration. Several others said they felt it too, but we didn't give it much thought."

The movement they

A giant wave, a tsunami, *struck Japan's eastern coast yesterday.*

were feeling was an earthquake occurring on the ocean floor. About an hour after Satoru felt the earth tremble, the water along the shore began pulling quickly out to sea. Midori Matsimoto was there. "There was a loud sound, like a 'boom!'" she said. "Then the water hissed as it was sucked out from the sand and rocks." Soon, the water being sucked out to sea started coming back—in a wave as tall as a seven-story building.

In moments, the enormous mountain of water swamped the coast, raging inland and smashing everything as it went. Seven-thousand fishing boats along the coast were destroyed. Villages all along the Sanriku coast were demolished, and thousands of people were swept to their deaths. With so little warning, most had no idea what hit them.

Fishermen out to sea returned to a scene of

(continued on page 2)

(continued from page 1)
destruction. "We barely felt the wave when it went under our boat," recalled Hikeki Isoroku, who'd been fishing when the wave hit shore. "That's the weird thing about tsunamis—they're huge and ferocious when they strike the coast, but when they're still moving out in the ocean, they're just a ripple."

Japan, with such a long and exposed coastline, has a long history of tsunami disasters. This one, the worst ever to strike the country, will no doubt spark intense research into these merciless marauders from the sea. Perhaps studying them will allow better preparation in the future.

TSUNAMI: THE SUMO WRESTLER OF WAVES

With Clay Marblerock, staff geologist

The word *tsunami* comes from the Japanese *tsu* (harbor) and *nami* (wave). Tsunamis are triggered by earthquakes on the ocean floor, which act like paddles, disturbing the water above the center of the quake and sending ripples out in all directions. (Some tsunamis are caused by meteorites that fall into the ocean.) Such waves, though very fast (they can move as quickly as 400 mph [644 km/h]), are barely noticeable at sea—they may be very small, hardly enough to rock a boat.

But as they approach land, they change—dramatically. The seafloor rises gradually as it gets closer to the beach, which forces the waves to slow down and concentrate their strength. They become monstrous walls of water, crashing upon coastal communities with incredible force.

MAKE YOUR OWN TSUNAMI

With Professor Cornelius

You have only to go as far as the nearest pond to witness how a tsunami works. Luckily, yours won't cause massive destruction!

You will need:
A pond and a rock

1. Find an edge of the pond where you can see the bottom.

   Pick a part of the pond with a "shore" that gradually slopes up to the surface.

2. Throw the stone some distance out from the shallow part—not too far from the edge, but far enough to get some good ripples going.

3. Watch what happens to the little waves as they race toward the shore.

   When the stone first strikes the water, the ripples are small. By the time they break onto the edge of the pond, they've increased in size from moving through the shallow water.

4. Next throw a bigger rock and REALLY have some fun . . .

Watch the ripples as they race away from the rock—what do you observe?

 # THE DAILY DISASTER

Sunday, September 9, 1900   Volume L No. 252   Price: 3 cents

TEXAS HURRICANE PROVES WORST IN U.S. HISTORY

Fierce cyclone surprises meteorologists

GALVESTON, TEXAS—"Everything's big in Texas," so the expression goes, and storms are apparently no exception. The hurricane that struck southern Texas yesterday was big enough to wipe this town virtually off the map. Estimates of the death toll are already approaching 8,000 (6,000 in Galveston alone), making it the worst disaster in American history to date.

The hurricane broke upon the Gulf of Mexico coast early yesterday. With a population of 38,000, Galveston is located on an island that amounts to little more than a sandbar. It is hardly surprising, then, that the hurricane's 15-foot (4.5-m) waves and 150 mph (241 km/h) winds left the community looking like it had been trampled by giants. More than 3,500 homes and buildings in the city and surrounding area have been flattened.

Galveston residents pick through the wreckage, hoping to find any belongings.

"There were warnings the previous week," recalled local newspaperman Hal Marleybone. "We got telegraph reports and firsthand news from sailors that a storm was roaring toward the Gulf of Mexico, after causing damage in Cuba and other parts of the Caribbean."

Although storm warning flags were raised over the harbor on the 6th, the local population remained unconcerned for the most part. In fact, one weather forecaster had already assured town officials that no hurricane could ever destroy Galveston. "As a result, less than half of the city's inhabitants bothered to evacuate before the storm struck," sighed Marleybone. Sightseers even came from as far away as Houston to observe firsthand the powerful surf that *(continued on page 2)*

(continued on page 2)

HERO OF THE WEEK:

Who is the climatologist who claimed that no hurricane could destroy Galveston? His name is Isaac Cline, of the U.S. Weather Bureau. His proclamation prevented Galveston from building a seawall to protect itself. But Mr. Cline did more than make up for his mistake. Early on the morning of the 8th, upon observing the worsening weather conditions, he sent a warning by telegram to Washington, D.C., then went by horse-drawn buggy down to the beach. There he rode back and forth among the many people gathered there to watch the storm, warning them to find safer ground. He saved many lives by this heroic and selfless act.

(continued from page 1)

began breaking on the beaches yesterday morning.

By 3 P.M. all of Galveston was submerged beneath seawater. The destruction would continue through the night. Safety was to be found in the wealthy neighborhoods. Galveston, home to a booming cotton export trade, was called the Jewel of Texas. The same bustling economy that had paid for the state's first post office, first telephones, and even a medical college had also created a fair number of mansions. It was within these sturdy buildings that many Galvestonians, rich and poor alike, found protection from the violent forces that raged around them. With their sturdy walls and expensive construction, these mansions could stand up to the windy storm better than other buildings.

But Galveston's wealth could do nothing to stop Nature's fury. Twelve city blocks, nearly three-quarters of the city, are in ruins. Virtually every survivor has lost a family member to the worst natural disaster in this nation's history. It's enough to make many of them wonder what other nasty surprises the new century has in store.

The U.S. Weather Bureau's storm tracker shows the path of the storm as it actually happened.

STORM WITH A MIND OF ITS OWN

With Hugh Midditee, staff meteorologist

The hurricane that demolished Galveston began its destructive career way out in the Atlantic Ocean, near the Cape Verde Islands, where a ship reported winds of about 25–30 mph (40–50 km/h) on August 28. By the beginning of September, the storm—which had not yet developed into a hurricane—was located about 200 miles (360 km) south of the island of Hispaniola. Soon it would reach Jamaica, where an entire stretch of railway was washed out by heavy rains. On September 3, Cuba got drenched by 12½ inches (320 mm) of rain in just 24 hours. Florida was next, where winds of 48 mph (77 km/h) were reported. It was around this time that the U.S. Weather Bureau in Washington, D.C., predicted in their infinite wisdom that the storm—very soon to become an actual hurricane—would turn north along the East Coast. Apparently nobody bothered to tell the storm this, because it instead headed west across the Gulf of Mexico on a path that no previous hurricane had taken. By the time it roared into Galveston it was as powerful as it was unpredictable.

THE DAILY DISASTER

Thursday, May 8, 1902   Volume LII No. 128   Price: 3 cents

CARIBBEAN PARADISE DISAPPEARS IN FIERY CATACLYSM

Volcano blankets town in burning ash

ST. PIERRE, MARTINIQUE—Mt. Pelee, on the Caribbean island of Martinique, towers over the nearby town of St. Pierre. At exactly eight minutes to 8:00 this morning, it turned against the town it has guarded quietly for more than 200 years, sweeping it away with an explosion of super-heated rock and ash. Now St. Pierre, looking more like a battlefield than the sunny coastal community it once was, is the final resting place of an estimated 29,000 victims—the worst volcanic disaster in recent memory.

The eruption did not come as a complete surprise to locals, who reported seeing steam rising out of the massive, cone-shaped peak as early as April 2. On the 23rd, light tremors were felt throughout the island, and from that day until today, irregular streams of smoke and ash were seen billow-

A plume of dust and soot covered the entire island of Martinique soon after Mt. Pelee's eruption this morning.

ing from the volcano. Yesterday, despite ominous rumblings from the mountain, the French governor issued proclamations denying that there was any cause for alarm.

He was wrong. Mt. Pelee's losing struggle with the forces that threatened to tear it apart finally ended this morning in an eruption of terrifying violence. Giant domes of molten rock exploded, sending a cloud of destruction hurtling down the slope of the volcano at tremendous speed toward defenseless St. Pierre 4 miles (6 km) away. Like an avalanche of super heated ash, the cloud covered the town in minutes, *(continued on page 2)*

(continued on page 2)

IN OTHER NEWS

ALL ABOARD!

Twenty-two-year-old inventor Joshua Lionel Cowen's new "Lionel" toy trains are all the rage with young engineers. Turn to TRENDS.

FULLER BUILDING PROGRESS REPORT

Check in on the status of what will be the world's tallest building. It's starting to look like a flatiron. See ART AND ARCHITECTURE.

CANAL: NICARAGUA OR PANAMA?

In Washington, senators wrangle over where to dig the U.S.-sponsored canal that will connect the Atlantic and Pacific Oceans. Turn to CURRENT AFFAIRS.

The streets of nearby villages have been covered in soot and ash; residents are getting out of town as quickly as they can.

(continued from page 1)

obliterating everything in its path. Only two survivors have been found, one of whom owes his life to the fact that he was in the relatively safe confines of a jail cell when the eruption occurred.

Little remains to remind the world that St. Pierre, now partially buried beneath layers of smoking volcanic spew, was once the largest city on this island. There is, however, something to forever remind us of the moment it ceased to exist: a clock has been found in the ruins of the local military hospital, stopped at the exact time of the destruction.

OUR READERS REACT

 Henrietta Monroe, 28, librarian:
"Why did the residents stay on the island after they heard it rumbling for so long? It seems to me that the government could have done more to evacuate them. There were warnings."

 Strom Everhard, 56, hotel bellhop:
"It just goes to show you what happens when you live next to a volcano. Folks should have sense enough not to go tempting fate like that."

 Roland McViney, 18, choir member:
"The world is a mysterious place, I reckon. At least those people were killed fast enough that they didn't have time enough to fret over their doom."

FANT**ASH**TIC TERMS!

With Professor Cornelius

Learn the different parts of a volcano, and you're on your way to being a real volcanologist!

Magma: molten rock that is still beneath the earth's surface

Lava: what molten rock is called after it has erupted from a volcano

Plume: the volcanic material that has erupted into the atmosphere

Obsidian: glass that is formed by rapid cooling of lava

Cinder cone: a pile of loose fragments that have accumulated around a volcanic vent

WHAT SCIENTISTS ARE CALLING IT

With Clay Marblerock, staff geologist

The 30,000 victims of Mt. Pelee were killed by what geologists call a *pyroclastic flow,* sometimes referred to as *nuée ardente* (French for "glowing cloud"). Composed of ash, deadly gases, and pumice (volcanic rock), they move like avalanches down the slope of a volcano after an eruption and can be as hot as 1500° F (816° C). Worst of all for those caught in their path, pyroclastic flows are fast; depending on the slope of the volcano and the strength of the eruption, they can sweep along at speeds of up to 450 mph (724 km/h). Needless to say, the citizens of St. Pierre didn't stand a chance.

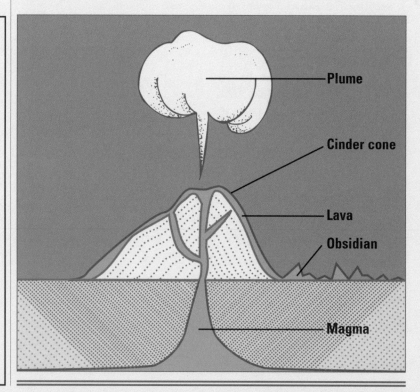

 # THE DAILY DISASTER

Saturday, April 21, 1906   Volume LVI No. 111   Price: 3 cents

TERRIBLE 2-FOR-1 TRAGEDY

San Francisco quakes, and gets burned in the bargain

SAN FRANCISCO, CALIFORNIA— The great city of San Francisco has vanished, replaced by a landscape of charred and broken ruins. Whatever was left standing after the earthquake of April 18 has been destroyed by three days of fire. Never

MESSAGE FROM THE MAYOR OF SAN FRANCISCO:

The Honorable E. E. Schmitz, mayor of San Francisco, has asked *The Daily Disaster* to print this proclamation in response to the criminal behavior that many have undertaken in his city.

The Federal Troops, the members of the Regular Police Force, and all Special Police Officers have been authorized by me to kill any and all persons found engaged in Looting or in the Commission of Any Other Crime.

before in modern memory has such a large and prosperous city been so completely wiped out.

A foreshock announced the coming calamity at 5:12 A.M. last Wednesday. The huge quake itself struck about 25 seconds later along the San Andreas Fault, and was felt as far away as Los Angeles and central Nevada. "San Francisco shook for almost a minute," said dock worker Robert Mandella, "but let me tell you, it seemed like a lifetime. Buildings collapsed like toy blocks, streets buckled like paper, and rifts appeared in the ground, swallowing whatever—and whomever—stood above them." Hundreds perished when their flimsy tenement buildings collapsed into the gaping earth. To add insult to injury, a major aftershock struck about three hours later, toppling many of the buildings that had managed

Houses tipped and tilted in an earthquake in San Francisco. These houses still stand—they are among the lucky few.

to survive the earlier quake.

But this was only the beginning of San Francisco's nightmare. According to police officer Jimmy McSwiggin, "As soon as the ground stopped its violent upheaval, fires broke out in almost every part of the city from exposed electric wires, overturned heating stoves, and broken oil lamps." Because the earthquake had severed virtually all of the city's water mains, many of the areas were without means of firefighting. Flames quickly raged out of control, gradually gathering into a giant blaze has lasted for three terrible days.

Although telegraph and *(continued on page 2)*

SO WHOSE FAULT IS IT, ANYWAY?

With Clay Marblerock, staff geologist

The tremendous earthquake that started this whole mess was the result of the ground moving along the notorious San Andreas Fault, a volatile stretch of shifting earth that runs roughly along the California coast. The quake ruptured the ground along the fault for a stretch of 290 miles (470 km), leaving a giant crack that has moved the earth as much as 25 feet (7.6 m) in certain places.

(continued on page 2)

(continued from page 1)
telephone lines within the city were cut by the quake, the postal telegraph operators were able to communicate with the outside world until they were evacuated at 2:20 P.M. on the 18th. As a result, U.S. Army and Navy personnel were alerted and ordered to the city to help fight the fire and tend to the wounded.

All over the city a valiant and desperate struggle has been waged by the city's firemen who have labored on despite exhaustion, hunger, and uncertainty as to the fate of their own families. Because of the frightful scarcity of water, buildings have been often dynamited in the hopes of stopping the inferno's advance.

Today the flames that swept through the Mission District were extinguished by 3,000 volunteers and a few firemen, marking what

A fireman helps a child out of the wreckage.

is hoped will be the last great battle against the burning enemy. Relief cannot come a moment too soon. Hundreds of thousands of victims must now face homelessness, as it is estimated that more than 28,000 buildings have been destroyed. The city faces losses in the millions of dollars. The death toll, still rising by the hour, has already exceeded 400. But worst of all is the knowledge that so many will never be found, their bodies having burned to ashes in the worst fire in American history.

THOUSANDS CHOOSE FLIGHT OVER BURNING

Almost immediately after the earthquake stopped its disagreeable rumblings, the Southern Pacific Railroad generously offered free passage out of San Francisco to those citizens wanting to make like a tree, and leave. Not surprisingly, many took them up on the offer. (Wouldn't you?) Since 6:00 A.M. on the 18th, the railroad has been transporting passengers out just as fast as they can, and they've given no sign of letting up. An estimated 200,000 people—out of a total population of 410,000—have already been railed to safety, making this one of the greatest evacuations in all of history.

A further 20,000 were evacuated from the waterfront yesterday by officers and men of the navy vessel USS *Chicago*, which had received word of the disaster in San Francisco by wireless communication from San Diego. This marks the first time that wireless telegraphy was used to help those caught in a natural disaster.

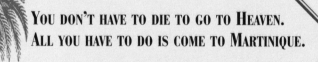
PLAY THE BUCKET BRIGADE!

To put out a fire when the fire trucks are empty, firemen sometimes create a line of people passing buckets of water to the scene of the fire. Try playing the Bucket Brigade with some friends and see how fast you can move the water!

What You Need:

Two buckets for every team

Paper cups for every player

Water

How to Play:

1. Divide into teams.

   Each team should have at least four people.

2. Fill one of each team's buckets with water.

3. Teams line up, with the full bucket at one end and the empty bucket at the other. Everyone grabs a paper cup.

4. The person nearest the full bucket fills her paper cup. These people are the captains.

5. The captains count to three and then shout "Go!"

6. On "Go," the captain pours the water out of his or her cup, and into the cup of the next person, who pours it into the cup of the next person, and on down the line until the last person dumps the water into the empty bucket.

7. Whichever team moves all the water to the empty bucket first wins!

THE DAILY DISASTER

Monday, April 15, 1912   Volume LXII No. 106   Price: 1 cent

TITANIC TAKES 1,500 WITH HER TO THE BOTTOM OF THE OCEAN

Iceberg does what nobody thought could be done

NEW YORK, NEW YORK—For a ship that nobody thought would ever sink, RMS *Titanic* did a very good job of doing just that. Late last night, she struck an iceberg in the North Atlantic and went to the bottom about 400 miles (640 km) off the coast of Newfoundland. It was her maiden voyage.

Titanic sailed out of Queenstown Harbor for the very first time on April 11. She was captained by E. J. Smith, who was known as

AND THE BAND 🎵 PLAYED ON 🎵

Titanic's band bravely played while the ship sank and frenzied passengers scurried across the deck. Incredibly, they continued to play even after their conductor, Wallace Hartley, gave them permission to leave and save themselves, exhibiting a rare sense of professionalism. But don't bother looking up their next record—every one of them went down with the ship.

The majestic Titanic sailed out of port April 11—just days later she would lay at the bottom of the Atlantic Ocean.

the Millionaire's Captain for good reason: aboard were some of the wealthiest Britons and Americans. Despite receiving warnings of icebergs from several other ships traveling in the North Atlantic, *Titanic* was to have a smooth and uneventful voyage.

Then, last night, the lookout rang the warning bell three times and telephoned the bridge at 11:40 P.M.: "Iceberg, right ahead!" Despite turning hard to the left, the giant vessel did not clear the ice, which scraped up against *Titanic*'s right

side for 10 seconds—a brief moment in time, but a fateful one.

Titanic's double-bottomed hull enclosed 16 watertight compartments. Because any four of them could be flooded (a remote possibility) and still not sink the ship, *Titanic* was considered unsinkable. But the collision had caused so much damage, five of the compartments filled with water. *Titanic* was doomed.

As the ship began to tilt dramatically to one side, panic spread amongst the passengers. Tragically, *Titanic*

carried only 20 lifeboats, enough to rescue less than half the ship's approximately 2,200 passengers. "People started arguing with each other on the crowded deck, pushing to get into the boats," recalls 46-year-old survivor Abigail Backstand, "Officers and crew could only barely maintain order, even though women and children were supposed to board first."

By 2:20 this morning, *Titanic* had slipped beneath the waves forever. With her went Captain Smith; ship designer Thomas Andrews, who had overseen *Titanic*'s construction; Ida and Isidor Straus, director of Macy's department store; the influential millionaire Jacob Astor; and more than 1,500 other unfortunate souls, most of whom were traveling third class, looking forward to a new life in America. *Carpathia*, another liner, had picked up *Titanic*'s (continued on page 2)

(continued from page 1)
distressed signal around midnight, and steamed at full speed to render assistance. By the time she arrived, around 4:00 A.M., only 705 passengers, in lifeboats, remained. All were picked up by *Carpathia* and taken to New York harbor safely.

Rescued passengers ride the Carpathia *to safety.*

HERO OF THE WEEK

Those who were lucky enough to get a spot on one of the lifeboats were eager to get away from the sinking ship—they knew that once the huge vessel went down the suction would pull any surrounding boats under. But one gallant woman defied the odds to take on passengers. Molly Brown, wealthy widow of Mr. James J. Brown of Denver, directed the rowing of her lifeboat and took on as many victims as she could despite the danger. Later, on *Carpathia*, she tended to the sick and dying. Survivors are already calling her the "Unsinkable Molly Brown."

FOLD A BOAT OF YOUR OWN!

 Start with a square piece of paper.

1. Fold it in half into two rectangles, then in half again. Unfold the second fold, but keep it folded in half once. Orient it so the crease is toward you.

2. Fold the lower right-hand corner up to the edge of the center and unfold it.

3. Fold the lower right-hand corner up to the crease you made in step 2.

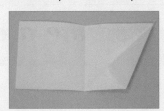

4. Unfold the paper until it is back to being square.

5. On the side without the small creases, fold the outside corners into the center of the square.

6. Leaving the corners folded in, fold the paper in half. It will sort of look like an envelope, with a triangle on top of a rectangle.

7. Fold the rectangle in half so the triangle is to the outside.

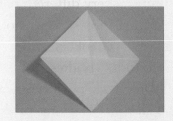

8. Fold along the small crease from step 3 behind the triangular part.

9. Turn up the point at the bottom and do a valley fold into the center of the boat.

10. Stand the boat up! It floats all on its own.

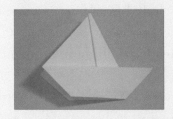

QUEEN OF THE SEAS

With Anita Holliday, staff travel correspondent

Built by Harland and Wolff shipbuilders in Belfast, Ireland, for the White Star line, RMS (Royal Mail Ship) *Titanic* and her sister ship, *Olympic* (that's right, there's another one still out there) are the largest moving objects ever created by humans. *Titanic* weighed a whopping 46,000 tons (42,000 metric tons), was propelled by three propellers that each spanned more than 16 feet (4.9 m), and sported four smoke funnels (although only three were needed—the fourth was added to make her look more impressive!). Her 16 watertight compartments were controlled by electric doors that could be opened and closed from the bridge.

Moreover, her builders lavished every luxury on her, from hardwood staircases to Italian Renaissance staterooms (for first class only, of course). The ship even boasted a Parisian-style café. With so much money and effort invested in her, she seemed impervious to the perils of the ocean.

THE DAILY DISASTER

Friday, July 9, 1918   Volume LXVIII No. 190   Price: 4 cents

101 KILLED IN NASHVILLE TRAIN COLLISION

Two locomotives take a one-way trip into each other

NASHVILLE, TENNESSEE— Dutchman's Curve, a stretch of railroad track just outside of Nashville, is surrounded on both sides by cornfields. But it is a very different harvest that greets the thousands of onlookers gathered there today: bodies.

Dutchman's Curve was the site this morning of the worst rail collision in American history. On this bend in the track, two trains collided head-on like metallic beasts in a duel to the death, resulting in an explosion heard 2 miles (3.2 km) away. Now, as the sun begins to set, some 50,000 people have gathered in the cornfields to offer assistance or to just gaze at the destruction. "What a mess," said 23-year-old nurse Jennifer Wypers. "Just a twisted jumble of steel, wood, and humanity sprawled on both sides of track. It is a grim sight indeed."

At 7:07 this morning, Engineer David Kennedy pulled the No. 4 train out of Nashville's Union Station, seven minutes behind

Crowds and survivors gather to take a peek at the destruction that once were the No. 4 and No. 1 trains.

schedule on a trip to Memphis. As he rumbled out of the station, the tower operator, J. S. Johnson, gave Kennedy a green signal, indicating that it was OK to proceed onto the single stretch of track that headed out of town toward Memphis. Johnson then realized that another train, the No. 1 coming from Memphis to Nashville, hadn't pulled into the station yet. It would have to use the same track the No. 4 was using.

Where was the No. 1? Thirty-five minutes late. Johnson, realizing his mistake, blew the emergency whistle, hoping to stop the No. 4. But apparently

nobody on that train heard it, because the No. 4 continued on, oblivious to its fate. Each train was now traveling around 60 mph (96.5 km/h) toward the other locomotive—on the same track.

When the two trains collided, the explosion rocked Nashville. One train "telescoped" the other—some of the lead cars of the No. 1 found themselves swallowed into the front cars of the No. 4. Other cars jumbled upon each other and derailed, littering both sides of the embankment. The trains were packed with factory workers and soldiers *(continued on page 2)*

(continued on page 2)

IN OTHER NEWS

SHE MAY NOT BE ALIVE, BUT SHE SURE HAS HEART

Popular new Raggedy Ann doll at the top of every little girl's wish list. See TRENDS.

AMERICAN TROOPS TO HAVE BORSCHT FOR CHRISTMAS DINNER?

President Wilson agrees to intervene in the Russian Civil War. See CURRENT AFFAIRS.

HIGH FLYERS GO POSTAL

Originally operated by the Army Signal Corps, the new airmail delivery service between New York and Washington, D.C., will soon be turned over to the U.S. Post Office. See THOSE MAGNIFICENT MEN AND THEIR FLYING MACHINES.

RAILROADS: HAVE THEY BECOME TOO DANGEROUS?

With Anita Holliday, staff travel correspondent

Many feel that buying a rail ticket these days is like taking your life into your own hands. Here are just some of the accidents that have occurred since the beginning of this century.

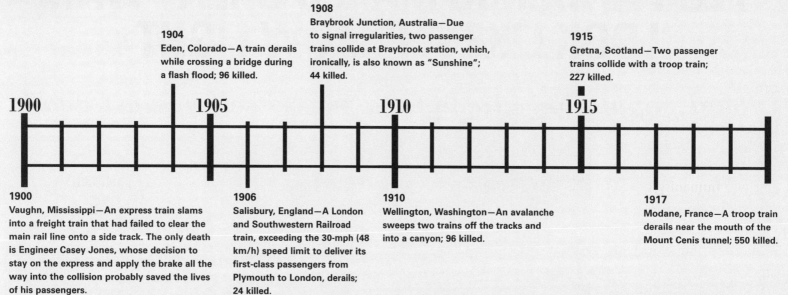

1904
Eden, Colorado—A train derails while crossing a bridge during a flash flood; 96 killed.

1908
Braybrook Junction, Australia—Due to signal irregularities, two passenger trains collide at Braybrook station, which, ironically, is also known as "Sunshine"; 44 killed.

1915
Gretna, Scotland—Two passenger trains collide with a troop train; 227 killed.

1900 | **1905** | **1910** | **1915**

1900
Vaughn, Mississippi—An express train slams into a freight train that had failed to clear the main rail line onto a side track. The only death is Engineer Casey Jones, whose decision to stay on the express and apply the brake all the way into the collision probably saved the lives of his passengers.

1906
Salisbury, England—A London and Southwestern Railroad train, exceeding the 30-mph (48 km/h) speed limit to deliver its first-class passengers from Plymouth to London, derails; 24 killed.

1910
Wellington, Washington—An avalanche sweeps two trains off the tracks and into a canyon; 96 killed.

1917
Modane, France—A troop train derails near the mouth of the Mount Cenis tunnel; 550 killed.

(continued from page 1)

en route to training camps.

"The destruction is horrific," said 19-year-old Nashville resident James Vickerby. "The wreckage looks like the result of some giant's temper tantrum. You can see corpses and body parts." Coffins are stacked nearby, awaiting excavation efforts to uncover the bodies, and dead wagons can be seen hauling corpses to already overcrowded funeral homes. It will probably be quite some time before citizens of Nashville decide to ride the rails again.

SURVIVOR OF THE WEEK

Robert D. Corbitt, brakeman for the Nashville-bound No. 1, managed to cheat death today, earning him the title of Survivor of the Week. After being knocked unconscious in the collision, he was found and declared dead. His body was sent to the morgue and was about to be embalmed when he awoke, proving his rescuers wrong. He is now receiving treatment in the hospital, and it looks like he's going to be just fine.

TRAIN YOUR MIND

With Professor Cornelius

Test your wits with this word problem. The answer may surprise you!

A train weighing 120 tons (122 metric tons) departs Chicago at 3:00 P.M. bound for Kansas City. Another train, weighing 160 tons (163 metric tons) departs Kansas City at 3:45 P.M., bound for Chicago. The first train, traveling at 50 mph (80 km/h), requires 600 feet (180 km) to come to a complete stop. The second train, carrying 300 tons (306 metric tons) of freight, requires 700 feet (210 km) to come to a complete stop. If both trains are on the same track, how far apart do they have to be to have enough room to stop without crashing into each other?

Answer: 1,300 feet (390 km) or more. All you need to do is add the distances the trains need to come to a stop. The rest of the information is not necessary.

THE DAILY  DISASTER

Sunday, December 1, 1918   Volume LXVIII No. 335   Price: 4 cents

FLU PANDEMIC MAKES GREAT WAR LOOK LIKE A PILLOW FIGHT

Global population attempts to mask itself against death

SAN DIEGO, CALIFORNIA—Less than a month ago, the worst war humanity has yet suffered finally ended. But instead of celebrating, people all over the world are dying.

A killer is among us. Unlike all the bullets and bombs that killed so many millions during the Great War, this is a silent killer. It can slay anyone in its path, whether wearing a uniform or not. It is airborne, it is invisible, and it has already murdered twice as many victims as the war itself.

You probably already know what it is, because virtually everyone on the planet knows somebody who has been infected. It is Spanish influenza. And it has developed into a pandemic (meaning worldwide epidemic)—the single worst disaster ever suffered by the human race.

Back in March, a soldier at Fort Riley, Kansas, reported into the infirmary with a sore throat, headache, and

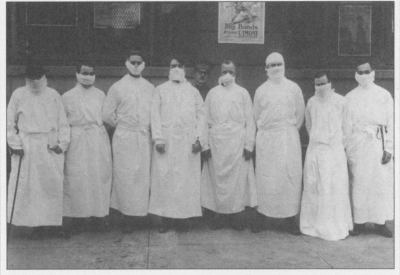

Protective gauze masks may help to keep the illness from spreading; doctors wear theirs at all times.

muscle aches—classic flu symptoms. Within a week, more than 500 people had it. Soon reports of severe flu were coming in from army and navy bases all over the United States. In a matter of months, every state in the nation has been affected.

"Symptoms are grievous and set in quickly," says San Diego surgeon Dr. Felix Abernathy. "Within a matter of hours, a healthy person can be debilitated by pains and weakness. Death may come soon after, and it's an awful way to go: the lungs fill

with blood, and the victim drowns in his own fluids."

When American soldiers were shipped overseas to take part in the war on the Western Front, they carried the silent killer with them, starting a domino effect that would circle the globe. By April, French soldiers were infected, as were people in China and Japan, and by May it had reached as far as South America. The virus swept through Spain like a whirlwind, where it got its name due to the extremely high mortality rate there.

AROUND *the* WORLD

EPIDEMICS *and* PANDEMICS

1141 BC:
Plague in Israel

1332
The Black Death, a plague, originates in India

1562
Plague in Paris, France

1665
Plague in London, England

1792
Bubonic plague in Egypt

1832
Cholera epidemic in United States

1918
Spanish flu worldwide

Perhaps most terrifying of all is that those most at risk are not the old and the infirm, but the young and the healthy. If you're between the ages of 15 and 40, look out—you're more likely to get it than your grandmother or baby sister.

(continued on page 2)

MAKE A DIFFERENCE: *THE DAILY DISASTER'S* "PUBLIC SAFETY HAIKU" CONTEST

In the interest of promoting health awareness, our staff is sponsoring a contest to see who can write the best Public Safety Message—the only restriction is that they must be haikus. A haiku is a simple three-line poem that doesn't have to rhyme, where each line has a certain number of syllables. The first and third lines have five syllables and the second one has seven. Here's an example:

> **The flu runs rampant**
> **Spreading sickness that's deadly**
> **Wear your mask or else!**

(5) _____

(7) _____

(5) _____

People everywhere are already creating messages to remind each other to be safe and wear their gauze masks—here are two of the popular ones, which you may have already heard:

> **Obey the laws**
> **And wear the gauze.**
> **Protect your jaws**
> **From septic paws.**

> **I had a little bird,**
> **Its name was Enza.**
> **I opened the window,**
> **And in-flu-Enza.**

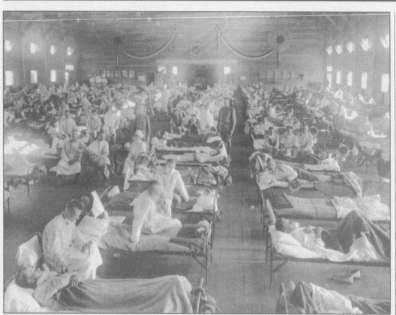
Sick wards are so overfilled with patients, empty warehouses are being used as makeshift hospitals.

(continued from page 1)
Do yourself a favor and heed the warnings of your local government about wearing a mask at all times. Here in San Diego, those failing to wear their masks in public are fined $100 and given seven days in jail.

The exact number of fatalities so far is impossible to know for sure, but it is certainly more than 20 million. Half a million people have died in America alone (200,000 just in October), which is nothing compared to other countries (over 80% of the Samoan population has been struck down). Nobody knows how it started, or how to battle it. Worst of all, nobody knows when—or if—it will end.

OUR READERS REACT:

Dick Lindahl, 37, banker:
"Well, now, I got to feelin' pretty rotten this morning. Got myself a headache and a sore throat. My body aches, too. Heck, I thought I was just comin' down with a little cold. You sayin' I might die? Is that what you're sayin'? Golly, you sure know how to bring a fella down."

Lydia Dornier, 45, schoolmarm:
"My husband Thomas came back from the war back in November. I was so happy to see him, so glad that he had survived the horrors of the Western Front. If you think I'm going to lose him now that he's home safe and sound, you've got another thing coming! I don't let him leave the house without his mask on, no matter how much he complains. He says I'm harder on him than his old sergeant!"

Phil Bucks, 52, barkeep:
"These masks they make us wear are drivin' me crazy. The cops will stop you right in the street if you're not wearing one! It's unconstitutional, I think. A person should have the right to do what he wants with his own face."

THE DAILY  DISASTER

Thursday, January 16, 1919   Volume LXIX No. 16   Price: 4 cents

MOLASSES FLOOD PUTS BOSTON IN STICKY SITUATION

Consequences of disaster anything but sweet

IN OTHER NEWS

NEW STYLE OF MUSIC TAKES OVER CHICAGO

Jazz can be heard throughout the bars and taverns of Chicago, which has overtaken the South as the new music's capital. See THE ARTS.

ROUGH RIDER

The Daily Disaster remembers the life and times of Theodore Roosevelt, whose funeral was held recently in Oyster Bay, Long Island. See CURRENT AFFAIRS.

PARIS PEACE CONFERENCE BEGINS IN 2 DAYS

World diplomats are due to arrive at Versailles, France, on the 18th to negotiate a peace treaty. See THE END OF THE GREAT WAR.

Knee-deep in sticky molasses sludge, firefighters attempt to clear the streets.

BOSTON, MASSACHUSETTS—It may very well go down as the oddest disaster in history. It certainly is the stickiest. Yesterday afternoon, a giant wave of molasses (yes, you read correctly) swept through the streets of Boston's North End, smashing buildings, killing 21 people, and injuring 150.

It all began at the waterfront facility of the Purity Distilling Company (owned by the United States Industrial Alcohol Company), where 2.2 million gallons (9.5 million L) of molasses were stored within a 50-foot (15-m) tall tank. "At around 12:30 yesterday afternoon, a deep rumbling noise shook the neighborhood, followed by the awful screech of ripping metal," said waterfront shop owner Jack Higgerdly. "All of a sudden that giant tank just burst apart into flying sheets of iron, releasing a thunderous wave of gooey, yellow-brown molasses. What a nightmare."

(continued on page 2)

WHAT CAUSED THE TANKS TO BURST?

With M. C. Squared, staff physicist

Rumor has it that the United States Industrial Alcohol Company was over filling the tank with molasses, which can be made into rum, a type of alcohol. Perhaps they were hoping to make as much as possible before Prohibition, the country-wide ban on alcohol, goes into effect next year.

A more likely cause involves the weather and simple physics. On January 12, the temperature was only 2° F (-17° C). The following day, just two days before the tank burst, the temperature rose to 40° F (4° C). This dramatic temperature change likely caused those 2.2 million gallons of molasses to expand uncontrollably, until the tank was not large enough to hold it all.

(continued from page 1)

Moving at tremendous speed, the sticky, 8-foot (2.4-m) wall of sugary destruction smashed everything in its path. The railroad buildings and freight sheds across the street were pulverized, rail cars and cargo sent sloshing into a brown oblivion. The wave, exerting a pressure of 2 tons per square foot (2.2 metric tons), crashed into the local elevated passenger train track, sweeping away a supporting trestle as if it were a Tinkertoy. Fortunately, a train had already passed the weakened stretch of track, which sagged into the muck below.

Soon the local firehouse was coasting off its foundation. Swept up by the flood, the structure sunk into the harbor. People and horses bobbed and struggled everywhere, helpless to free themselves from the pasty deluge, now thick with the debris of ruined buildings.

Almost as soon as the waves of molasses had subsided, officers and men of the vessel *Nantucket*, anchored nearby, arrived on the scene to offer assistance to the wounded. Army troops soon followed.

Today, firemen started cleaning up the awful mess, which covers two city blocks. "Apparently, fresh water is no good at washing away the sticky stuff," says 24-year-old fireman Bob Haskell. "So we're pumping seawater onto the buildings and wreckage. It'll take us weeks to get this job done."

There has been no comment as of yet from the United States Industrial Alcohol Company. But many in Boston believe that their offices will soon be thick with lawyers in search of a sweet compensation.

The destroyed molasses tanks that caused so much trouble.

MOLASSES: GOOD FOR MORE THAN JUST DESTROYING THINGS

So what is molasses? Well, molasses is made from the refining of sugar cane and sugar beets. The juices are boiled down to a syrup, from which sugar crystals are extracted. This leaves you with a thick dark liquid—molasses.

Just so you don't think molasses only kills people, we present this recipe for molasses cookies. Other delicious foods, including gingerbread, shoofly pie, or Boston baked beans also contain molasses.

MOLASSES COOKIES

Ingredients

4 cups all-purpose flour

$\frac{1}{2}$ teaspoon salt

$2\frac{1}{4}$ teaspoons baking soda

1 tablespoon ground ginger

$1\frac{1}{4}$ teaspoon ground cloves

$1\frac{1}{4}$ teaspoon cinnamon

1 stick ($\frac{1}{2}$ cup) unsalted butter, softened

$\frac{1}{2}$ cup vegetable shortening

3 cups sugar

$\frac{1}{2}$ cup molasses

2 large eggs

For cookie coating:

$\frac{1}{2}$ cup sugar

1. Preheat oven to 325° F (293° C). Lightly grease two large cookie sheets.

2. In a large bowl whisk together the flour, salt, baking soda, ginger, cloves, and cinnamon.

3. In another large bowl beat the butter, shortening, and sugar with a mixer until light and fluffy.

4. Beat in molasses.

5. Beat in eggs one at a time, beating well after each addition.

6. Gradually beat in flour mixture until well combined.

7. In a small shallow bowl put remaining $\frac{1}{2}$ cup sugar. Form dough into 2-inch balls and roll in the sugar. Arrange balls on baking sheet approximately 4 inches (10 cm) apart and flatten slightly.

8. Bake in the middle of the oven for 15 minutes or until puffed and golden. Transfer to wire rack to cool. Cookies should be soft.

Makes approximately 25 cookies.

THE DAILY  DISASTER

Thursday, March 19, 1925   Volume LXXV No. 78   Price: 4 cents

TRI-STATE TWISTER DOESN'T KNOW WHEN TO QUIT

Hundreds killed by monster tornado

MURPHYSBORO, ILLINOIS— A giant twister cut a path of destruction through parts of Missouri, Illinois, and Indiana yesterday afternoon before it finally called it quits. By the time the interstate calamity was over, 19 separate communities had been blown apart with the loss of nearly 700 lives—the worst ever for a single tornado.

It first touched down around 1:00 P.M. near Ellington, Missouri, where it began moving in a northeasterly direction. After blowing through the communities of Annapolis and Leadanna, the cyclone charged across Bollinger County on its way to the Mississippi River. Leaving 11 people dead in Missouri, it crossed over into Illinois, slamming into Gorham around 2:30 P.M. and adding another 34 deaths to its tally. One survivor was Ernest Schwartz, a cashier at Gorham's First Illinois

This house was found after the tornado left—it may have been carried as far as ten miles by the twister.

National Bank. Upon hearing the roar of the approaching tornado, he took shelter in the vault— along with almost all of the bank's money. He emerged later to a scene of utter ruin.

After leaving the stunned folks of Gorham, the tornado went on a 40-minute rampage through a whole slew of communities, killing 541 people and injuring more than 1,400. Worst hit was the poor town of Murphysboro, where the storm left a fire in its wake and fully half the town is

either dead or injured. In all, some 600 citizens of Illinois have perished.

Indiana was next on the agenda. The twister crossed its second river this day at the Wabash, turning the town of Griffin upside down. It went on to destroy 85 farms and half the town of Princeton. Then, mercifully, like a galloping horse that's finally spent, the tri-state twister petered out and dissipated 10 miles (16 km) northeast of Princeton. Behind it, in a straight line *(continued on page 2)*

(continued on page 2)

"OH, GIVE ME A HOME WHERE THE BUFFALO (AND TORNADOES) ROAM . . ."

With Hugh Midditee, staff meteorologist

More tornadoes occur in the United States than in any other country—about 800–1,000 per year. The highest concentration touch down in the central and southern plains states of Kansas, Oklahoma, and Texas, usually in the spring and summer. They form inside large thunderstorms when changes in wind speed and direction create a spinning, funnel-shaped motion. Their winds can blow in excess of 300 mph (480 km/h), like the tri-state monster you just read about, although most of them barely peak at 100 mph (160 km/h), which is still powerful enough to uproot small trees or push a motor car off the road.

The funnel cloud picked up everything in its path as it wandered through Missouri, Illinois, and Indiana yesterday.

(continued from page 1)

running southwest to northeast for over 200 miles (322 km) there are 695 deaths, more than 2,000 injured victims, and 15,000 ruined homes.

Clearly, this was no ordinary tornado. "That thing must've been a mile wide," claimed 50-year-old eyewitness Helga Fitzroy. Its average forward speed was over 60 mph (96 km/h)—most tornadoes travel at around half that speed. Between Gorham and Murphysboro it was clocked at 73 mph (117 km/h)! And, worst of all, it stuck around for a frightening 3½ hours.

Here in Murphysboro, the fire department was unable to fight the flames that consumed much of the town after the twister came through. "The water supply was cut by the twister," said fireman Alexander Woosh. "Most of the 234 fatalities here are victims of the fire."

Even for people who are accustomed to the threat of tornadoes, this was an unbelievable nightmare—one they certainly hope never to see again.

SURVIVING A TORNADO
With Sergeant Safety, staff safety consultant

You won't have much warning before a tornado strikes—maybe someday in the future, when fancy computing machines have been invented, weather forecasting will become advanced enough to predict them ahead of time (but we doubt it). Should you be unlucky enough to encounter any of these spinning marauders from the sky, try to remember these survival tips:

Keep an eye out for
- Dark, often greenish sky
- Large hail
- Loud roar—
  it sounds like an approaching freight train

If it looks like a twister is heading your way, don't try to outrun it—you've got a better chance of discovering the Emerald City in Oz than you have of out distancing a twister. Get to your granny's jam cellar in a hurry. If you can't find a basement, make for a room on the ground floor of a building. Get to the middle of the floor, hide under a sturdy piece of furniture, and roll yourself up into a ball.

MAKE A VORTEX IN A JAR!

With Professor Cornelius, Jr.

 What You Need:
A tall glass jar
Water
Spoon
Food coloring

 What You Do:

1. Fill the jar with cold water.

2. Using the spoon, stir the water around quickly. Keep the spoon near the surface of the water and try to make the water spin as quickly as possible.

3. Watch for the vortex to appear. Add a few drops of food coloring to the center of the surface and it will take the shape of the funnel!

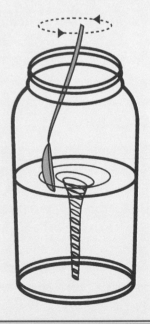

THE DAILY  DISASTER

Wednesday, June 1, 1927 — Volume LXXVII No. 152 — Price: 5 cents

MISSISSIPPI MADNESS MAKES MAYHEM FOR MILLIONS

Worst flood in American history creates hordes of homeless

IN OTHER NEWS:

BABE RUTH

Although it's early to say for sure, Babe Ruth has a chance at beating the 59-home run per season record this year. See SPORTS.

UNDERWATER MARVEL

Engineers are scheduled to complete construction of Holland Tunnel this year, connecting New York City with New Jersey. See PROGRESS.

SUPER TOYS?

Scientists claim to be on the verge of creating a new plastic called *polystyrene,* whose toughness will be ideal in the manufacture of toys. See TECHNOLOGY.

BATON ROUGE, LOUISIANA— The mighty Mississippi River may be the lifeblood of the country, but it also has a mean streak. The river is now 80 miles (130 km) wide in some places after the worst flooding this country has ever seen.

"Noah would feel right at home," said 50-year-old Jed Edmondson, whose hometown of Greenville, Mississippi, has been practically washed away. "The water came a-crashing through, carrying houses away. I don't know how we'll ever recover." From Cairo, Illinois, to the Gulf of Mexico, the Mississippi River system has become one long, giant lake. Fully 26,000 square miles (67,000 sq. km) of land in seven states have been inundated by water.

It has certainly come as no surprise to weather forecasters. Last year's autumn saw record rainfall across the nation—in northwestern

The water keeps rising, making streets and parking lots look more and more like swimming pools by the minute.

Iowa alone, 15 inches (38 cm) of rain fell in three days during September. The winter was even worse. December 13 was a grim day for South Dakota— the temperature fell 66° F (34° C) in 18 hours, after which a terrible storm dumped piles of snow. Conditions were similar across the Midwest.

Then, as if adding insult to injury, the spring rains came with a vengeance, adding their torrents to the rivers already flooded with melted snow. The Illinois

River (which flows into the Mississippi) at Beardstown, Illinois, was already at flood levels by September last year—it remained there throughout the rest of the year and is still there now.

By April of this year, the levees along the river could no longer contain the high water. All along the Missouri, Arkansas, Mississippi, and other rivers, work crews— mostly black men—worked frantically to heap sandbags on top of the levees, making them higher and more able *(continued on page 2)*

Secretary of Commerce Herbert Hoover

(continued from page 1)

to withstand the rising water. In 120 different places, their efforts were in vain, unleashing fierce floods that crashed through the levees and swamped the surrounding land.

The levee at Mounds Landing, Mississippi, is a good example of what was happening all through the river's system. There, hundreds of black men who had been pressed into service by local authorities tried desperately to build up the wall that held the Mississippi at bay. Then, at 12:30 P.M. on April 21, the whole thing gave way, releasing a thunderous wall of water that swept into the region known as the Mississippi Delta. There was no hope of stopping it.

The death toll, in excess of 300 people, is difficult to estimate with total accuracy. Hundreds of people in rural areas have either perished or gone missing. Nobody knows how many black workers have been drowned by the broken levees on which they were working. It is known that at least 500,000 people have been made homeless. Many of these individuals have been aided by the Red Cross, sent in by Secretary of Commerce Herbert Hoover. Hoover, whose quick action has earned him the admiration of millions, is already considered a viable candidate for President of the United States.

HERO OF THE WEEK

When the levee at Mounds Landing broke, chaos followed. As soon as the levee gave way, hundreds of black workers sought shelter on a nearby barge in the river, trying to get away from the raging torrent that was flowing through the breach. A tugboat, attempting to push the barge downstream, was actually straining against the suction created by the water flying past the broken levee. One of the white men on the tugboat suggested cutting the barge loose, leaving all the blacks on it to a gruesome fate. Charlie Gibson, an old and feeble contractor, piped up, "We ain't goin' to cut the barge loose," he ordered. He went on to say that he'd shoot anyone who tried. "If we go, we go together," he barked.

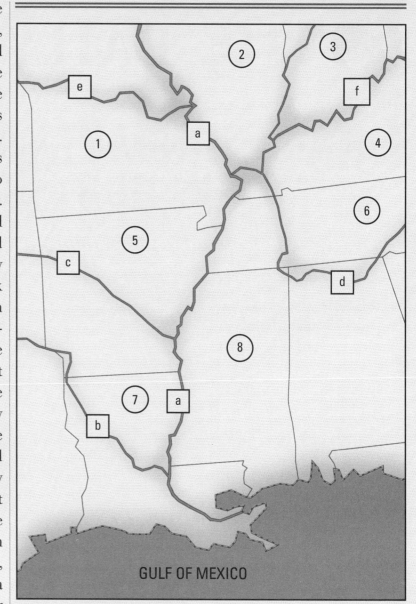

GULF OF MEXICO

THE BIG PICTURE

With Professor Cornelius, Jr.

Just to give you some idea of how much area has been socked by this terrible disaster, we've provided the map above. You have to do the rest of the work, however. Can you name the states and rivers most affected by the flood? States are numbered, and rivers have letters.

Answer Key:

a Mississippi	f Ohio	5 Arkansas
b Red	1 Missouri	6 Tennessee
c Arkansas	2 Illinois	7 Louisiana
d Tennessee	3 Indiana	8 Alabama
e Missouri	4 Kentucky	

THE DAILY DISASTER

Sunday, April 14, 1935 | Volume LXXXV No. 104 | Price: 5 cents

"BLACK SUNDAY" WORST DAY YET IN DUST BOWL

Gigantic cloud of filth rolls across Kansas

DODGE CITY, KANSAS—Here in the southern plains, it's no coincidence that *dust* is a four-letter word. The worst dust storm to occur since the beginning of the drought in 1931 blew across the plains today, causing widespread damage and leading many to start calling this area the Dust Bowl.

In the four years since the drought's onset, more than 75% of the United States has been affected, making it the worst in the nation's history. In Kansas, Oklahoma, Colorado, and Northern Texas, the drought has brought a particularly unpleasant feature with it: dust storms, giant clouds of sandy grit that are picked up by strong Midwest winds. They have steadily increased in number and frequency each year, but none compares to the great black blizzard that struck Dodge City today.

"The morning had been clear and sunny," said resident Patsy Glynn. "People glad for a break from the

An enormous storm of dust and dirt enveloped Dodge City, Kansas, today.

blowing dust were taking advantage of the agreeable weather to attend Palm Sunday services, hang their laundry, or just chat." Shortly after noon, the temperature dropped in only a few hours from around 90° F (32° C) to below 50° F (10° C). Everywhere, birds began stirring noisily, as if they knew that something terrible was on its way. Then around 2:30 in the afternoon, eyewitnesses saw a gigantic, black, billowing wall approaching the area around Dodge City from the west.

It struck like a cold, swirling dirt storm, pushing tons of tiny dust particles before a cutting wind. As the cloud rolled over the landscape 7,000 feet (2,000 m) high, it blotted out the sun, destroying even the slightest visibility. Soon everything was as black as night. Motorcars turned on their headlights to no avail, and pulled off the road or ran right into each other. Others had to stop—the static electricity generated by the tiny moving particles shorted out their engines.

(continued on page 2)

THOUSANDS LEAVE DUST BEHIND FOR HOPES OF A BETTER LIFE

It's not just huge clouds of blowing sand that people out here have to face. With the Great Depression in full swing, farmers are losing their land—which isn't producing anything anyway—to bank foreclosures, and jobs are scarce. Dust storms are just the final nail in the coffin for many who've decided to head west to find something better. At the rate they're moving, it may well turn into the largest migration in American history. Many are heading for California, where they hope to find work as migrant laborers on huge corporate-owned farms. We spoke with Grandpa Joad, who said, "Jus' let me get out to California where I can pick me an orange when I want it. Or grapes."

(continued from page 1)

Nowhere was it possible to escape the blowing dust. For more than three hours the black storm raged, swallowing the area into darkness and filth. By the time the winds stopped blowing in the early evening, Dodge City and its surrounding countryside had been covered with a blanket of dust. It was everywhere: sloping up against houses and sheds, covering fences, filling cars, and burying tractors. It was piled on cupboards, beds, floors, and tables. Nothing and nobody was spared on what everyone is calling Black Sunday.

Behind masks of grime, the weary folks of the Dust Bowl look at each other and wonder how many more seasons of this horror they will to have to endure. And still there is no rain in sight.

PLAY THE DUST BOWL GAME!

With Professor Cornelius, Jr.

Pretend you're caught in the dust storm and have to round up all your friends and family! You can't see because the dust is so thick—we'll use a blindfold for that—and everyone else is caught somewhere else and can't find their way back, either.

What you'll need:

Blindfold

At least four friends

How to Play:

1. Blindfold one person.

   This person is the one in charge of rounding everyone up.

2. Everyone else runs away and hides.

3. The blindfolded person shouts out "Dust!" and hidden people answer "Storm!"

4. Based on sound alone, the blindfolded person tries to find all of the hidden people!

WHERE DID ALL THIS DUST COME FROM?

With Forrest Greenacre, staff ecologist

For years, farmers in this part of the country have been over using the soil. Only now are they beginning to understand that methods of farming that worked back East don't work in the Midwest, where the soil is drier. Irresponsible agricultural practices have left the ground dried out and depleted of essential minerals. The drought has sucked the last bit of moisture out of the ground and left a layer of worthless sand. Fierce winds off the wide, flat plains kick up all that dust into storms that make life miserable.

THE DAILY DISASTER

Friday, May 7, 1937   Volume LXXXVII No. 127   Price: 2 cents

HINDENBURG GOES DOWN IN HISTORY, UP IN FLAMES

Giant airship mysteriously explodes while attempting to dock

LAKEHURST, NEW JERSEY—Yesterday, disaster struck as the German transatlantic airship *Hindenburg* blew up in Lakehurst. More than 35 passengers are feared dead.

Hindenburg, the largest hydrogen-filled, rigid airship ever built (for that matter, the largest object ever built) and pride of the Nazi regime in Germany, left Hamburg on May 3 with 97 passengers and crew. By the evening of the 5th it had completed an uneventful crossing of the Atlantic and turned south, following the coast of Canada. It flew back and forth over New York City around 3:00 P.M. on the 6th, after which it proceeded on to New Jersey.

At 7:00 P.M. the zeppelin made its approach toward the giant mooring post, a tower that stretched into the sky and allowed zeppelins to pull alongside and tie themselves for docking. Fifteen minutes later, it began to reverse its

People watched in horror yesterday evening as Hindenburg *exploded into flames in Lakehurst.*

engines and descend. Mooring ropes were being dropped off the right side when it was about 260 feet (79 m) in the air and perhaps twice that distance from the mast. Then it happened.

"A gigantic plume of fire burst violently from within her, lighting up the evening sky," recalls 33-year-old teacher Mac Puxtallone, there to see the famous zeppelin's arrival. In seconds, the entire length of the hydrogen-filled vessel was

bright with searing flame, its stern starting to sink while smoke billowed upward. "*Hindenburg* had become a floating inferno," said Puxtallone. Passengers, some of them on fire, leapt to the earth, many to their deaths. Those on the ground did not know whether to run for their lives or to stay on behalf of the poor victims they saw spilling out of the wreckage. As the dying ship settled to the ground, its metallic *(continued on page 2)*

(continued on page 2)

IN OTHER NEWS:

WAR RAGES IN BARCELONA

The Fascists and the Communists take their conflict to Barcelona, where ugly street fighting has broken out. See SPANISH CIVIL WAR.

DARING FLIGHT AROUND THE WORLD

Courageous aviator Amelia Earhart plans around-the-world flight. See MAKING HISTORY.

IT'S THE FAIREST OF THEM ALL

Read our review of the first feature animated film, Walt Disney's *Snow White and the Seven Dwarfs*. See FILM & THEATER.

(continued from page 1)

skeleton shone for a moment against the blazing destruction. Then the whole thing slumped into a smoldering ruin.

In all, it all took barely more than 30 seconds. Many survivors either walked out of the wreckage as soon as it hit the ground or were helped out by navy personnel from the naval air station. Of the 35 deaths, most are crew members. *The Daily Disaster* wonders, in the face of this tragedy, has the age of the zeppelin come to an end?

TAKING LUXURY TO NEW HEIGHTS

With Anita Holliday, staff travel correspondent

Ever since Count Ferdinand von Zeppelin started promoting their construction back in 1900, large rigid airships have held the promise of affordable, rapid transportation. *Hindenburg*, named for the famous German general of the Great War, was the first transatlantic airliner and represented the finest in zeppelin design. At 804 feet (245 m) in length and 135 feet (41 m) in diameter, it had a range of 8,000 miles (12,874 km) and could cross the Atlantic Ocean in just 50 hours (compare that to a ship, which could take weeks, and you realize why people were willing to pay $400 a ticket!). Even the food served on board was special: fresh Black Forest brook trout, venison cutlets Beauval with Berny potatoes, and tenderloin steak with goose liver sauce were just some of the airship's scrumptious offerings—all of which, sadly, are now quite overdone.

WHAT WENT WRONG?

It is too early to tell whether a gas leak or a bolt of lightning is responsible for destroying the largest air vehicle ever built. We may never know. However, rumors are already circulating that *Hindenburg* may have been sabotaged. We will provide more details as they come to light.

THE DAILY DISASTER

Thursday, November 7, 1940 | **Volume XC No. 312** | **Price: 10 cents**

GALLOPING GERTIE GIVES UP THE GHOST

Infamous dancing bridge crumbles to pieces

TACOMA, WASHINGTON—At 11:10 this morning, only four months after opening to the public, the Tacoma Narrows Bridge collapsed into Puget Sound. Casualties include one automobile, a dog, and the confidence of American bridge engineers.

Authorities closed the bridge to traffic at 10:00 A.M., alarmed by winds that blew in excess of 40 mph (65 km/h), making the bridge oscillate (wave) violently. Eyewitnesses claim the road lurched as much as 11 feet (3.3 m), causing one of the cable bands to loosen and slip out of place. Just over an hour later, a 600-foot (183 m) stretch of the span's structure broke apart in a dramatic and thunderous fall to the water below.

The action that shook the bridge to pieces came as no surprise to local residents, who had already nicknamed the span Galloping Gertie. Since opening on July 1, the bridge became renowned for its dance routine, caused by even light winds blowing across the sound. Motorists caught at such moments

The Tacoma Narrows Bridge crashed into Puget Sound this morning.

were treated to a free roller coaster ride, at times heaving high enough to obscure sight of the cars ahead.

"The Tacoma Narrows Bridge was originally built to replace the ferry, once the only way to get across Puget Sound between Tacoma and Gig Harbor," said school teacher Bernie Fox. "With a center span of 2,800 feet (853 m), it was the third largest suspension bridge in the world—until today." Designed by Leon Moisseiff, whose plan gained favor for its affordability (estimates came in at under $7 million), the bridge saved money and

gained its streamlined appearance by making the girders 8 feet (2.4 m) deep, approximately one-third the standard depth. The affordable solution proved disastrous.

Once ranked among the prestigious American landmarks that included New York's George Washington Bridge and San Francisco's Golden Gate Bridge, the structure's new claim to fame may well be its spectacular failure: with more than 5 times the raw materials of *Titanic*, the Tacoma Narrows Bridge is the largest man-made structure ever to be lost at sea.

IN OTHER NEWS:

"IT'S A BIRD! IT'S A PLANE!"

It's Superman! Listeners everywhere are tuning in to the Man of Steel's new radio show. See ENTERTAINMENT.

HOW DO THEY DO IT?

Everyone's talking about the amazing new science of television, first demonstrated in New York by CBS, the Central Broadcasting System. See TECHNOLOGY.

FLYING OFF THE SHELVES

Originally designed to help aircraft manufacturers sell their products to the military, model airplanes have suddenly become popular among the younger set. See TRENDS.

The last person to step foot on the late, great Tacoma Narrows Bridge was Howard Clifford (photo at top), who raced onto the bridge in an attempt to save a dog. Leonard Coatsworth, a Tacoma newspaper editor, had been driving along the bridge when the structure's movement made him lose control. He got out of the car (the only vehicle on the bridge), and was promptly thrown to the pavement. As the sounds of cracking pavement and metal sounded, he made a dash to the car in order to rescue his dog Tubby. Unable to reach the car, he crawled for the safety of the toll plaza. Clifford raced onto the bridge, but the violent motion tossed him from side to side, and he was forced to retreat. Tubby, sadly, went down with the car as Galloping Gertie fell apart.

Incredibly, the whole episode was captured on film, and we have permission to print a photo here.

WHAT MADE GALLOPING GERTIE GO GONZO?

With M. V. Squared, staff physicist

One theory involves a concept called *resonance*. You can see resonance in action by tapping a tuning fork and holding it next to a guitar's strings, some of which will begin vibrating. They'll do this because their frequency is the same as the frequency of the vibrations being sent out by the tuning fork—they're in resonance. You can also see resonance in action when an opera singer makes a glass shatter with the sound of her voice. In the case of Galloping Gertie, the winds that were blowing across Puget Sound created disturbances that were at the bridge's natural frequency, resulting in resonance, which made the whole bridge vibrate dramatically, twisting the road and putting terrible stress on the cables. The stronger the winds, the greater the vibrations, and—crash! The cables were pulled from their moorings, releasing the roadway to fall to its doom.

BUILD YOUR OWN BRIDGE!

Using only plain white glue and uncooked spaghetti, try to build a bridge that can sustain the weight of three encyclopedias.

You can use as much spaghetti as you want, but try to use as little as possible!

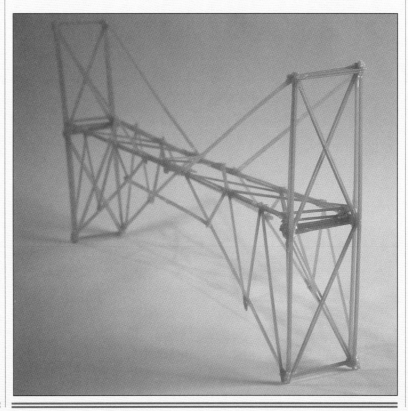

LOCAL RESIDENTS REACT

Peter Holzenherger, 14, student:

"Before the bridge came along, we never had any fun around here. Ridin' ol' Galloping Gertie was swell! Now what are we gonna do for fun? Play kick the can? Ever play kick the can? What a bore."

Bertha Futz, 41, housewife:

"Who cares about a bridge? The Nazis are overrunning Europe, and we're worried about a defective bridge? At least we live in a country where we can build another one in peace."

Martin Estees, 56, physics teacher:

"We should pass laws that require bridge builders to be more cautious and to put their designs through elaborate tests. Maybe they should put models of their designs in a wind tunnel, or something, before constructing the real thing."

The Daily Disaster

Thursday, January 11, 1962 | **Volume CXII No. 11** | **Price: 10 cents**

Avalanche Crushes Thousands in Peru

TONS OF SNOW FILL MOUNTAIN VALLEY TO THE BRIM

RANRAHIRCA, PERU—The word *snow* reminds most people of holiday parties, snow fights, and shoveling the driveway. But to many people in Peru, it now means something much, much deadlier. Yesterday, a gigantic avalanche swept like white death through a canyon in the Andes Mountains, obliterating villages and killing thousands.

Nevado de Huascarán is the second highest mountain in the Andes range, which runs the length of South America. On January 9, a large storm dumped tons of snow onto the slopes of the peak.

Yesterday, all that snow began to melt, sending sheets of water down into the glacier that lay beneath it, weakening it. An afternoon of this was more than the glacier could take, and at about 6:15 in the evening, disaster struck.

Several tons of snow and ice broke loose, falling 3,000 feet (914 m) into the valley below. "There was a deep, loud rumbling sound," said 28-year-old Diego Montoya, whose village lay right in the avalanche's path. "It sounded just like what a battle must sound like from a distance. It was quite terrifying."

Terrifying, indeed. The massive white wall was traveling at incredible speed, picking up enough momentum to crash through buildings as if they were made of paper. The villages of Pacucco and Yanamachito were annihilated,

The valley floor of the Andes mountains flooded when the snow and ice atop Nevado de Huascarán broke loose and came crashing down.

adding their rubble to the frozen flood.

It took only five minutes for the avalanche to cover nine miles (14.5 km) of valley, wiping out four more villages on its way to Ranrahirca.

More than 50 feet (15 m) high, moving at greater than *(continued on page 2)*

(continued on page 2)

IN OTHER NEWS

JOHNNY WHO?

Some guy named Johnny Carson to become new host of *The Tonight Show* this coming fall. See ENTERTAINMENT.

ROCKET MAN

Read our interview with Lt. Col. John Glenn, who's scheduled to make the first American orbit around Earth next month. See SPACE RACE.

LOSING FACE

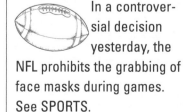

In a controversial decision yesterday, the NFL prohibits the grabbing of face masks during games. See SPORTS.

Peru, on the western coast of South America, is home to Nevado de Huascarán, the second highest mountain in the Andes mountain range.

WHEN GOOD SNOW GOES BAD

With Harry Kane, staff meteorologist

Everybody loves to play in snow (it sure beats sitting in it). But the fact is, snow—when it's on hills or mountains—can be really dangerous stuff. Here's why.

When fresh snow falls, it can make the old snow beneath it unstable. If the older snow is hard and crusty, its surface can be slick and slippery, making an ideal surface for the heavy new snow to skid and start an avalanche. Another danger involves what are called *depth hoar* crystals, also known as *corn snow*. These form in the bottom layers of snow pack when vapor is exchanged between snow and the ground it sits on. The snow crystals grow to as much as five times their previous size and become unstable. Because the density of corn snow layers is less than the density of snow above them, they can be forced to move and set off an avalanche.

Sometimes an avalanche will occur when loose snow piles up. Loose snow, in which the individual crystals fail to bond to each other, behaves like sand. Disturb some of it, and layers will start moving down the slope, gathering speed as they go.

When you put all these conditions onto a steep slope, you've got a disaster just waiting to happen. Even the slightest vibration will set it off. The resulting cascade of snow may look harmless enough from a distance, but it is anything but—it's moving at tremendous speed, and can uproot trees, smash buildings, and bury people alive.

GET MOVING
With Professor Cornelius, II

As described by *The Daily Disaster* meteorologist Kane, some avalanches can occur when loose snow behaves like sand. To see how this happens, you don't need a snowstorm—just a sandbox.

1. Form sand (not dirt) into a pile about a foot high. Make sure it's stable.

2. Fill a bucket with more sand.

3. Tip the bucket just enough to spill a trickle of sand, and gradually pour the sand from the bucket onto the "hill" beneath.

Try to do it so that the hill doesn't start cascading down its slopes (it's not easy!). You can imagine that the sand you're pouring is new snow, and the hill is old snow that—if you're not careful—could get moving and turn into an avalanche. See how much sand you can pour onto the hill without creating any movement.

(continued from page 1)
100 mph (160 km/h), the avalanche pushed a zone of compressed air before it. This dense, fierce air slammed into communities like a hurricane before the ice and snow even arrived. "It was awful, simply awful," said 40-year-old survivor Felipe Mendes. "We heard a terrible roar, then out of nowhere came this incredible wind, blowing everything to pieces. Before we knew which end was up, the snow and ice came, destroying and burying everything. I can't believe I'm alive."

Survivors are now working to dig through the snow. They hope to find any buried survivors and personal belongings, but the odds are stacked squarely against them. Hopefully, no more snow will arrive to complicate the rescue efforts.

All along the valley, snow has replaced villages and towns.

The Daily  Disaster

Saturday, November 5, 1966   Volume CXVI No. 309   Price: 10 cents

Arno River Becomes World's Harshest Art Critic

ART DESTROYED ALONG WITH 100 LIVES IN FLORENCE

Residents in Florence are swimming, not walking, to the aid of museums, whose priceless works of art are at risk of getting drenched.

FLORENCE, ITALY—Today, the great Italian city of Florence mourns the loss of some 100 lives—and countless pieces of art. The fearful damage was caused by the Arno River, which overflowed its banks and soaked the city in some of the worst flooding it has ever seen.

Heavy rainfall across southern Europe was responsible for flooding many rivers across the region. Sometime around 2:30 A.M., the Arno River began sending waves of floodwater toward Florence at an estimated 36 mph (58 km/h). By 4:00 A.M., water had swept into the city's main square. "It was a lousy way to start the day, let me tell you," said 58-year-old Vito Vinchezzi, a store owner on the Ponte Vecchio, where many of the city's famed gold and silver shops are located. "I was awakened at around 3:00 A.M. and told that my merchandise might be ruined unless I got down there and started hauling the stuff out to safety. What a mess!"

By 7:00 A.M., the city had been cut off from the rest of the country. Florence's sewer system was incapable of handling the massive influx of water, and raw sewage started filling the streets. Worse, oil tanks burst open, filling the floodwaters with great, black oil slicks.

Florence is home to some of Europe's largest and most valuable art collections. With a filthy goo of water, oil, and sewage filling the streets (it is estimated that more than a million tons of silt have been deposited throughout the city's buildings), many of these priceless artifacts have been ruined beyond repair. Among the lost treasures are frescoes by Botticelli, Pietro Lorenzetti, Simone Martini, and Paolo Uccello. Historic documents, musical instruments, and arms collections have also been lost. It is one of the worst calamities ever suffered by the world's antiques and art community.

(continued on page 2)

IN OTHER NEWS:

STAR POWER

Movie star Ronald Reagan doing well in race for governor of California. See POLITICS.

TV: IT'S NOT JUST FOR WATCHING ANYMORE

Engineer Ralph Baer claims that it may be possible to design games that can be played on your television. See TECHNOLOGY.

WHERE NO MAN HAS GONE BEFORE . . .

Viewers give mixed reviews of new television series *Star Trek,* in which a spaceship whips around the universe seeking contact with alien life forms in the 23rd century. See ENTERTAINMENT.

Mud and muck coat the floors inside museums, churches, and every other building in town. People are trying to clean it up as quickly as they can.

BE AN INTERNATIONAL RIVER EXPERT!
With Frank O'File, staff linguist

Learn to speak about rivers, floods, and water no matter what country you're in! Practice them and then teach your friends!

Language	Water	River	Flood
Chinese	shui (shway)	hu (hoo)	hongshui (hong-shway)
French	eau (oh)	rive (reeve)	inondation (een-ohn-day-shuhn)
German	wasser (vah-sser)	fluss (floos)	uberfluten (oo-bear-floo-teh)
Hebrew	mayim (my-am)	nachal (nakh'-al) or nahar (naw-hawr')	mabool (ma-bool)
Italian	acqua (ah-kwah)	fiume (fyoo-may)	alluvione (ah-loo-vee-oh-nay)
Japanese	mizu (meet-tzu)	kawa (kah-wah)	shinsui (sheen-shwee)
Russian	voda (va-da)	reka (rey-ka)	navodneniye (na-vad-nyen-i-ye)
Spanish	agua (aag-wah)	rio (ree-o)	inundacion (een-oon-dah-see-on)

(continued from page 1)

Many of the city's residents are angered by the government's handling of the disaster. "It seems that city officials didn't want to send up an alarm so early in the morning," said 30-year-old Maria Bollo, who, along with many other Florentines, has been helping to carry artworks and historic documents to safety. "We should've been warned as soon as they knew about the rising water. Now we've lost irreplaceable artifacts. It's as if a large part of our past has been destroyed."

APPEAL FROM THE CITY OF FLORENCE:

A CALL TO ARMS!

NO, WE'RE NOT TALKING ABOUT THE SORT OF ARMS THAT SHOOT BULLETS, BUT THE ARMS THAT SPROUT OUT OF YOUR SHOULDERS. WE NEED THEM! THE THOUSANDS OF PRECIOUS ARTWORKS, BOOKS, MANUSCRIPTS, AND OTHER VALUABLES THAT MAKE THIS CITY SUCH A WONDERFUL PLACE ARE IN DANGER OF BEING LOST TO THE FLOOD. WITH YOUR HELP, WE CAN EVACUATE THEM FROM THE WATER AND TAKE THEM TO HIGH GROUND. HUNDREDS OF YOUNG PEOPLE FROM ACROSS ITALY HAVE ALREADY FLOCKED HERE TO VOLUNTEER THEIR EFFORTS. THIS ISN'T JUST FLORENCE'S DISASTER—IT IS THE WORLD'S DISASTER; AT STAKE IS THE CULTURAL HERITAGE OF EUROPE. PLEASE, COME TO FLORENCE AND LEND A HAND (OR TWO)!

—BROUGHT TO YOU BY THE FLORENTINE MINISTRY OF ANTIQUITIES

HERO OF THE WEEK

The Italian government may have been asleep on the job, but at least one concerned citizen wasn't. Romeldo Cesaroni is one of Florence's night watchmen. Early this morning, when the waters started inundating the streets, he took it upon himself to help save the city's precious gold and silver collections that line the Ponte Vecchio. Using a bicycle as transportation, he rode from house to house, waking the shop owners whose stores were threatened with destruction. Because of his efforts, artisans were able to run to their shops and transport their valuables to safety. His quick thinking has saved the city of Florence an incalculable amount of treasure.

The Daily  Disaster

Saturday, November 14, 1970   Volume CXX No. 318   Price: 15 cents

Enormous Cyclone Smashes East Pakistan

HUNDREDS OF THOUSANDS FEARED DEAD IN CENTURY'S WORST WEATHER-RELATED DISASTER

CHITTAGONG, EAST PAKISTAN—Just after midnight yesterday morning, a cyclone crashed into the coast of East Pakistan. High winds, torrential rain, and a massive storm surge all turned this South Asian country into a war zone. Over 300,000 people have been killed—nothing like it has been seen in the 20th century.

The storm system formed over the Bay of Bengal, an area notorious for cyclones. By November 11, the storm was 650 miles (1,046 km) southeast of Chittagong, boasting 75 mph (121 km/h) winds. As it moved northwest, communities along the coast of East Pakistan saw the waters of the bay rising ominously. "The water began washing away homes along the coastline," recalled 32-year-old survivor Abdul Sarita. "It just kept getting higher and higher, washing further inland. All we could do was try to find high ground."

Then, early on the morning of the 13th, the storm itself arrived, sweeping into the coast off Jaffrabad. Winds blowing at

Hundreds of people, now homeless, stand knee-deep in the floodwaters that destroyed their homes.

139 mph (224 km/h) blasted homes apart and sent debris flying. Worst of all, the storm surge lifted the water 10 to 15 feet (3.4 to 4.5 m) higher than normal, flooding huge stretches of countryside and further demolishing communities. Buildings, people, animals, and trees were swept away by pounding waves and rising seawater. "I couldn't believe my eyes," said 60-year-old Shakti Varma, who, along with several fellow survivors, managed to find safety on a relatively high hill. "So many corpses filled the water, rushing past. I must have counted over 200 head of cattle in the water."

In fact, over 1 million livestock are missing, and the raging sea has claimed more than 1.1 million acres (445,000 hectares) of rice paddies. Worst of all for this poor nation, hundreds of thousands of tons of grain have been washed away, virtually ensuring that famine will soon follow.

On islands just off the coast, entire villages have vanished, leaving no survivors. Hundreds of boats have been beached and can be seen lying inland, far from the ocean. From the trees hang all manner of rubbish and debris, as well as bodies. It is a sobering sight indeed.

IN OTHER NEWS:

HELTER-SKELTER

Millions of rock fans the world over still haven't recovered from the breakup of the Beatles this past April. See MUSIC.

MONKEYING AROUND

Moviegoers across America give the *Planet of the Apes* sequel *Beneath the Planet of the Apes* a lukewarm reception. See ENTERTAINMENT.

SONGBIRDS

ABC's new TV show *The Partridge Family* steals primetime ratings with its mix of music and comedy. See TELEVISION.

MAKE A STORM SURGE AND SEE FOR YOURSELF

With Professor Cornelius II

What You Need:

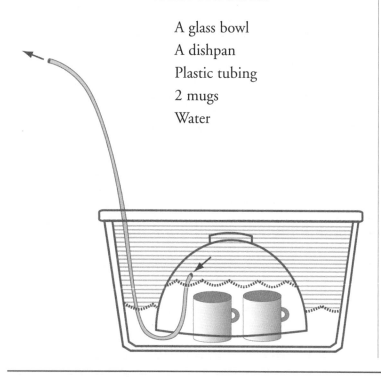

A glass bowl
A dishpan
Plastic tubing
2 mugs
Water

How to Make a Storm Surge:

1. Fill the dishpan half full of water.

2. Stand the cups upside down in the pan and place the bowl upside down on them.

   The rim of the bowl should be below the water's surface. Add more water to the pan if necessary.

3. Pinch the end of the plastic tubing so water doesn't get in, and push it under the water and up again so that it opens into the air space in the bowl.

   Stop pinching the end of the tube once it's in place.

4. Suck some of the air in the bowl through the tube.

   You'll see the water level inside the bowl rise.

5. Remove the tubing.

6. Lift the bowl to release the water, and you'll see a storm surge in action!

PSYCHO ABOUT CYCLONES

With Wayne DeLay, staff meteorologist

A cyclone is a huge storm that revolves around a center of low pressure. If it occurs in the Northern Hemisphere, it's called either a hurricane or a typhoon, and it spins counter-clockwise. If it forms in the Southern Hemisphere, it's called a cyclone, and it spins clockwise. The monster that hit East Pakistan yesterday started in the Southern Hemisphere (even though nearly all of its victims lived in the Northern Hemisphere), so it's called a cyclone.

Although high winds and heavy rain are extremely dangerous, one of the worst aspects of a cyclone is what's called the *storm surge*. This happens when the cyclone's wind and pressure raise the ocean water beneath it. Storm surges can be more than 15 feet (4.5 m) in height, leading to massive flooding as the water surges inland when it hits the coast. In a country like East Pakistan, thousands can drown as a result.

This storm surge reached a height of 16 feet.

THE DAILY ☠ DISASTER

Wednesday, July 28, 1976　　　　　Volume CXXVI No. 210　　　　　Price: 15 cents

Big Trouble in Middle China

Members of the army, armed with pickaxes instead of weapons, race to Tangshan to help dig the city out from under the rubble.

TREMENDOUS EARTHQUAKE TURNS MAJOR CITY INTO RUBBLE

TANGSHAN, CHINA—Talk about a rude awakening. At 3:42 this morning, an extremely powerful earthquake shook the city of Tangshan, China. The estimated number of deaths has already hit 250,000, making it the deadliest earthquake of the 20th century.

Tangshan, an industrial city of 1 million people, was asleep when the quake hit. Measuring an impressive 7.8 on the Richter scale, it ripped the city apart for almost 16 seconds, burying victims in their own homes before most of them had a chance to wake up and find cover. By the time the earth had stopped shaking, Tangshan had been completely leveled. Then, this afternoon, a powerful after shock—measuring 7.1 on the Richter scale—finished off what was left.

Oddly enough, there had been warnings that a disaster was coming. In a nearby village, well water rose and fell three times yesterday. Other wells throughout the region showed signs of cracking, and one even sprouted oil three days ago. Stranger warnings also occurred: Chickens ran around excitedly, refusing to eat; a goldfish was seen jumping out of its bowl; mice ran around, hurriedly looking for out-of-the-way places to hide. Some people even reported hearing loud noises and seeing lights and fireballs crossing the sky.

(continued on page 2)

SHAKE, RATTLE, AND ROLL

With Shale Marblerock, staff geologist

Our understanding of earthquakes goes hand-in-hand with the science of *plate tectonics*. The earth's crust is composed of giant plates, which, when moving, can scrape against each other. The plate on which the Indian subcontinent sits is moving in a northeasterly direction, while the Philippine plate and Pacific plate are both pushing westward. The city of Tangshan, despite being hundreds of miles from these plates, sits on land that is squished between them. Like a piece of paper that can wrinkle in the middle if you push on its edges, the region around Tangshan is reacting to forces that build up pressure from a great distance away, creating a fault. When the pressure in this fault becomes strong enough, the sides of the fault slip against each other, releasing tremendous energy. That's when you get an earthquake.

CHINA, NO STRANGER TO QUAKES

Because of its complicated geology, China has been a favorite haunt of earthquakes since time immemorial. Back in A.D. 132, a man named Zhang Heng invented the first *seismometer*. He fitted a large jar with ornamental dragons on the outside, each of which held a ball that would be released if an earthquake struck. Opposite each dragon was a frog with its mouth open, which would catch the released ball and thereby indicate which direction the ground was moving.

(continued from page 1)

Tangshan is now a ruin. Seventy-eight percent of industrial buildings and 93% of residential buildings are completely destroyed. Fourteen percent of the sewerage pipes are damaged. Even the water supply has been cut. As if this wasn't enough, all but one of the roads into Tangshan have been made impassable because of rubble and large cracks in the ground, creating a traffic jam of emergency vehicles. Relief and recovery will be slow in coming.

"Tangshan was not considered to be at very grave risk of an earthquake," claims local official Liu Changshe. "As a result, unfortunately, buildings in the city were not built to sustain a quake as powerful as the one that leveled it this morning."

As soon as the quake ended, citizens of Tangshan set about digging out the dead and the wounded. There is hope that emergency vehicles will be able to get to the city within the week.

WHAT YOU SHOULD DO DURING AN EARTHQUAKE
With Captain Caution, staff safety consultant

If you're inside, stay there. Move into a hallway or get up against an inside wall. Crawl under your desk if you're at school. Stay clear of fireplaces, windows, and heavy furniture. Don't run downstairs or outside while the building is shaking, and don't even THINK of going near the kitchen—it's a very dangerous place to be during an earthquake. If you're outside, things are a lot simpler: just get away from anything that might fall on you, such as buildings or power lines. Stay in the open. If you're in a car, slowly pull off to the side, as far away from bridges and overpasses as you can get, and stay in the car until the shaking stops.

MAKE YOUR OWN SEISMOMETER
With Professor Cornelius III

Be the first person on your block to know when a quake is coming. A seismometer is an earthquake detector, and you don't have to be a geologist to make one! Here's a simple seismometer that will allow you to detect movements in the ground.

What You Need:

A large cardboard box

String

Scissors

A small but heavy object (a building block will work)

A felt-tip pen

Tape

A clean sheet of paper

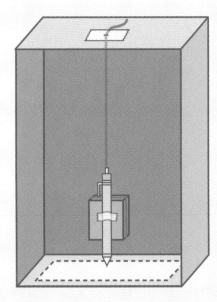

Build a Seismometer!

1. Cut an arm's length piece of string.

2. Tie one end of the string to the block.

3. Tape the pen to the block, uncapped, so that the tip hangs below the block if you hold the string.

   Make sure the pen is upright and sturdy.

4. Cut off the opening flaps of the box and turn the box onto its side. (The opening should face you.)

5. Cut a hole in the box in the side which is now on top.

6. Thread the string through the hole until the block and pen are hanging from the top of the box and the pen just barely touches the bottom.

7. Tape the string to the top of the box to hold the position.

8. Slip a clean piece of paper under the pen.

9. Stomp around the box!

   Check on the paper to see what happens when movements shake the box! You'll be able to see the effects of an underground rumbling—and maybe even make some art!

THE DAILY ☠ DISASTER

| Saturday, July 18, 1981 | Volume CXXXI No. 199 | Price: 25 cents |

Hotel Causeway Crashes Kansas City Party

POOR CONSTRUCTION TURNS ATRIUM INTO KILLING GROUND

KANSAS CITY, MISSOURI— Some 2,000 people were gathered at the Kansas City Hyatt Regency yesterday for a dance contest when two walkways collapsed onto the main level lobby. With 114 people dead and more than 200 injured, this is one of the deadliest structural failures in American history.

A tea dance brought the crowd to the hotel last night. "The live big band music provided by the Steve Miller Orchestra had everybody moving," recalled 20-year-old survivor Gladys Puffin, "and a carnival atmosphere pervaded the Hyatt's huge, state-of-the-art atrium lobby." At around 7:00, the band started playing "Satin Doll," and those who weren't dancing to the song's medium tempo were tapping their feet and keeping time. Most were on the ground level with the band, but plenty stood watching and swaying on the hotel's "skyways"—walkways suspended from the ceiling above.

The central atrium of the Kansas City Hyatt Regency is in ruins today, after a causeway collapsed last night.

At 7:05, a terribly loud cracking noise rudely interrupted the big band music. The topmost skyway came loose, fell into another one that was two stories beneath it, and sent both crashing onto the ground floor. "Needless to say, it brought the festivities to an abrupt and extremely unpleasant conclusion," said 40-year-old saxophone player David "Tex" Argyle.

Although this is the sort of thing you'd expect from some weakened old relic, the Kansas City Hyatt Regency—owned by the Crown Center Redevelopment Corporation —is only a year old. Begun in spring of 1978, the 40-story hotel features cutting-edge design concepts, the most celebrated of which is its massive atrium, enclosing 17,000 *(continued on page 2)*

(continued on page 2)

IN OTHER NEWS:

THINK TWICE BEFORE BUYING AN AIRLINE TICKET

 As American air traffic controllers threaten to strike, airports across the country panic. See CURRENT AFFAIRS.

NEW MILESTONE FOR WOMEN

 Read our interview with Sandra Day O'Connor, who recently became the first woman nominated to the United States Supreme Court. See GOVERNMENT.

FIGHTING CONTINUES IN THE MIDDLE EAST

As the Iraqi offensive slows to a grinding halt, Iranian resistance continues to grow. See IRAN-IRAQ WAR.

(continued from page 1)
square feet (1,584 sq. m). In fact, yesterday's disaster was not the first time the hotel had trouble. On October 14, 1979, while the hotel was still under-construction, 2,700 square feet (251 sq. m) of the atrium roof collapsed. Apparently, one of the roof connections at the atrium's north end had failed.

Interestingly, Crown Center Redevelopment Corporation, the hotel's owner, is owned by Hallmark, Inc.—who will no doubt be selling a great many sympathy cards in the wake of yesterday's catastrophe.

FAULTY CONSTRUCTION OR RECKLESS DANCING?
With Moe Mentum, staff physicist

There are plenty of theories as to why a hotel that's been open for only a year could experience such a disastrous structural failure. Some speculate that the band's music sent up vibrations at a frequency that loosened the walls from which the skyways were suspended. This is pretty far-fetched—we're talking about an orchestra here, not AC/DC. Another theory focuses on the dancers themselves, whose movements atop the skyways may have shook them enough to pry them loose. If this is so, then the problem lies not with the unfortunate dancers, but with the hotel's construction—which brings us to the most likely cause of the disaster.

Although a thorough investigation has yet to be made, it appears that as a result of confusion created by a lack of communication between the engineering firm and the steel corporation hired to build the atrium skyways, the original construction plan was abandoned in favor of a weaker one. As a result, the skyways weren't capable of bearing the proper—and legal—amount of weight. It was only a matter of time before they gave way.

OUR READERS REACT:

Isaac Spool, 43, machinist: "How new was this hotel? Brand new, wasn't it? How does something like this happen? I think the builders should be held responsible. Isn't there a way to test structures like this before they're opened to the public?"

Susan Flacker, 33, artist: "It doesn't surprise me. It seems everyone's out just to make a buck these days, to get everything done as quickly as possible. They leave out the details, don't pay enough attention, and—wham!—somebody gets hurt in the end."

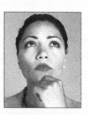

Sharon McMullan, 25, professional athlete: "I've never trusted hotels, anyway. People should stay in bed and breakfasts. They're so much more personal."

DON'T MAKE YOUR NEXT DANCE PARTY A DISASTER!

We wouldn't want any of our readers to be called a wallflower at their next social gathering. Toward that end, we're offering the following simple instructions for one of dancing's most timeless forms, the Foxtrot. Make sure you move the furniture to a safe distance before practicing!

Start with the basic forward step, then onto the basic backward step, then rock, turn, and start over from the beginning. These are the man's steps—since he faces the woman, she would do each move backward. Follow the numbers and try it out for yourself.

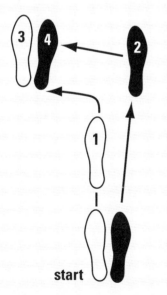

BASIC FORWARD STEP

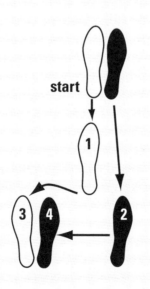

BASIC BACKWARD STEP

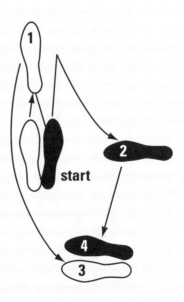

ROCK, TURN

THE DAILY ☠ DISASTER

Sunday, July 17, 1983 | Volume CXXXIII No. 29 | Price: 25 cents

Brush Fires in Australia Give New Meaning to "Ash Wednesday"

HIGH WINDS WHIP UP FURIOUS FLAME FEST

MELBOURNE, AUSTRALIA— Yesterday, Ash Wednesday in the Christian calendar, a new record was burned into Australian history: 10 brush fires broke out in the states of Southern Australia and Victoria, setting 865,000 acres (350,000 hectares) ablaze and killing 76 people. It is the worst bout of brush fires ever to have occurred in Australia.

Like so many disasters around the world recently, the cause can be traced back to that enormous annoyance of the Pacific: the weather pattern called El Niño.

The drought caused by El Niño that started in April of 1982 turned the southern reaches of Australia into a giant bed of kindling just waiting to be lit. The brush fire season is at its peak in that region, and when fires broke out yesterday, weather conditions conspired to fuel the flames until they raged out of control.

The immediate causes of each individual blaze are not presently known—reflected

High winds knocked down signs and destroyed buildings, and the fires the wind scattered across the country burned everything in sight.

heat from broken glass, careless barbecuing, and even arson are feared to have contributed. Extremely low humidity, around 10%, made things worse, but the single greatest contributor to the inferno was a cold front that crossed southern Australia from the southwest.

Its effect was twofold: First, it created a zone of high winds that succeeded in fanning the fires and driving them at speeds of up to 100 mph (160 km/h); and second, after it passed, wind direction made

an abrupt shift, transforming the fires from narrow scorching corridors into broad burning fronts that whipped across the dry, flammable countryside.

In conditions like these, escape can be nearly impossible, as the flames move so quickly and change direction so unpredictably. Worse, as the gusts picked up, many individual fires merged. The conflagration that flared up near the town of Clay Wells, Southern Australia, burned up 300,000

(continued from page 1)

EL NIÑO STRIKES AGAIN

With Wayne DeLay, staff meteorologist

Every so often, an upwelling of warm water in the equatorial Pacific Ocean is strong enough to severely alter water temperatures and air pressures. The effect is called El Niño, and it can have an impact on weather conditions clear across the globe. The El Niño that started last year is one of the severest in history, screwing up weather patterns all over the place. While some regions of the world have experienced torrential rain and flooding, others have been stricken with drought—including Australia, which is why so many fires started yesterday and got so rapidly out of control. It's an amazing example of how closely related all the regions of the earth really are. It's not just a small world— it's also a small atmosphere.

USE PLANTS TO TRACK HUMIDITY!

With Professor Cornelius III

One of the major reasons that the fires got so large, so fast, was that the humidity was very low. Now you can tell if the air around you is humid or not by taking note of plants that may be around your house!

Acorns: an acorn will close up tightly if it's really moist out, but if the humidity drops, the acorn will start to open up.

Dandelions: the flowers of a dandelion are only open when the air is dry—if it's humid they remain closed.

Seaweed: kelp and bladderwrack, two types of seaweed, are susceptible to changes in humidity: if it's humid out, their leaves become soft and bendable, but if it's dry, they become brittle and shriveled.

(continued on page 2) acres (120,000 hectares), making it the single greatest fire in history.

In Victoria's heavily forested Otway ranges, 729 homes went up in flames. Refugees flocked to nearby beaches, where they spent the night waiting for the fires to burn out.

Thirty-three-year-old Tracy Dodds was one of the few survivors: "All we could do was huddle on the sand, watching the smoke over us," she said. "The beach was scattered with ash. Everything smelled like smoke."

In the end, a total of over 2,500 houses were destroyed, thousands of livestock and other animals were killed, and incalculable millions of dollars have been lost in damages. Added to all this are the 76 people who died. Luckily, the conditions that set the stage for these fires don't come around all that often.

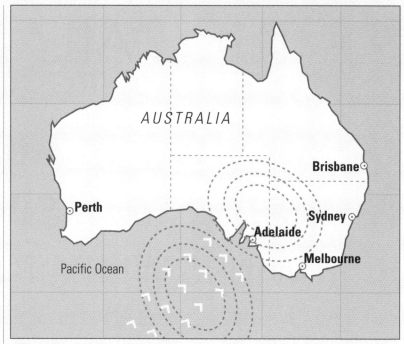

The El Niño weather pattern caused strange wind patterns, which sent bush fires into towns all along the coast.

SOME LIKE IT HOT

With Autumn Greenacre, staff ecologist

Of course, when your house is burning down and your backyard looks more like the top of a birthday cake than a lawn, you're probably in no mood to appreciate the necessity of fire. Nevertheless, Australia needs fire just as much as it needs water or sun. Take one of Australia's native plants, for example. Heath Banksia (*Banksia ericifolia*), a funny-looking plant with an orange flower-spike that can be up to 24 inches (60 cm) long, has a rather cozy relationship with fire. Heath Banksia seeds are stored within a tough, woody cone that can be opened only by the extreme heat of flame. Moreover, the seeds won't even grow if their parents are still standing—unless the ranks of the older generation get thinned by fire, the next generation can't begin.

THE DAILY ☠ DISASTER

Tuesday, December 4, 1984　　　　Volume CXXXIVI No. 48　　　　Price: 25 cents

History's Worst Chemical Disaster Kills Thousands in India

UNION CARBIDE PLANT SENDS CLOUD OF DEATH THROUGH BHOPAL

BHOPAL, INDIA—Last night, a huge volume of deadly chemical gas leaked out of a storage tank in Union Carbide's Bhopal plant. Thousands were killed in what is surely the worst industrial accident in history.

Methyl isocyanate, otherwise known as MIC, is an extremely dangerous chemical used in the production of pesticides. Unfortunately, its primary victims on this occasion weren't creepy-crawly bugs.

Since 1969, Union Carbide India, Ltd., has maintained a plant in Bhopal for the production of MIC. It was planned as part of India's "green revolution" to strengthen the subcontinent's agricultural output. At 11:30 last night, workers in the facility reported burning and tearing in their eyes. It soon became obvious that water had leaked into the overfilled MIC storage tank #610, resulting in a dangerous chemical reaction. By the time the plant supervisor reacted to his employees' reports, some two hours after

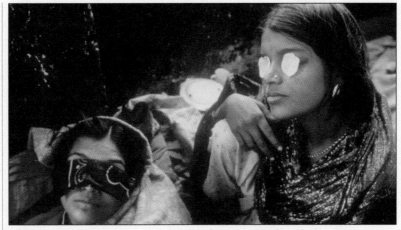

MIC, methyl isocyanate, leaked into the town of Bhopal, damaging residents' eyes, throats, and lungs, and killing countless others.

initial complaints, roughly 40 tons (36 metric tons) of MIC had poured out of the tank. The gases were driven as far as five miles (8 km) by the wind into Bhopal, a city of 900,000 people.

Because MIC is heavier than air, it remains close to the ground, creeping along the earth. "The unsuspecting people, most of them asleep, had no warning of the horror that enveloped them," said local resident Nanda Bhoopalam. "It was terrifying! Thousands were killed outright, a figure that will almost certainly rise due to the tens of thousands who now

suffer in the aftermath." Their symptoms are numerous and grisly: damage to the eyes, throat, and lungs; an inability to concentrate; and loss of motor skills. The worst horrors are yet to come, as India's medical facilities are not equipped to care for so many gravely injured by such a rare and little-understood sickness.

The vast majority of those affected were living in the crowded shantytowns that surround the Union-Carbide plant; almost all of them are—or were—extremely poor. Tragically, recent newspaper *(continued on page 2)*

(continued on page 2)

(continued from page 1)

articles had warned the residents of these areas that an accident could occur at the facility, and that they were all at tremendous risk. The warnings were mostly ignored.

As soon as word reached Union Carbide's headquarters in Connecticut, United States, CEO Warren Anderson pledged to fly directly to the site of the disaster with a technical team to aid in clean-up and relief. The Indian Government, however, isn't likely to welcome his arrival with open arms—word is already out of their intention to either place Mr. Anderson under house arrest or throw him out of the country (perhaps both).

Map of India

AFGHANISTAN

PAKISTAN

CHINA

NEW DELHI

NEPAL

○ BHOPAL

BANGLADESH

CALCUTTA

INDIA

BOMBAY (MUMBAI)

ARABIAN SEA

BAY OF BENGAL

INDIAN OCEAN   INDIAN OCEAN

GROUND TRAVELING AIR
With Professor Cornelius III

Heavy, toxic air traveled along the ground and brought death to thousands of people in Bhopal. You can see for yourself how layers of air can travel by using another substance: water! In this activity, you'll see how layers of water can behave differently from each other.

Cold water sinks just like heavy air does—see for yourself!

What you need:
  Ice

  Aluminum foil sheet

  Food coloring

  Water

  Flat, shallow glass dish (like a baking dish)

See Cold Water Move:

1. Fill the glass dish with hot tap water.

   Let it sit until the water becomes still.

2. Wrap some ice cubes carefully in the foil so that there are no gaps. Place the foil package at one end of the glass dish, in the water. Let the dish sit until the water becomes still.

3. Place a few drops of food coloring on the foil so that they drip into the water. Watch the color sink to the bottom of the dish and travel across its length!

   Because the food coloring is cold when it enters the water, it immediately sinks to the bottom!

UNION CARBIDE: Not exactly running a tight ship in Bhopal
With Moe Mentum, staff physicist

The fact that MIC tank #610 was filled beyond its proper storage capacity is just one of the mistakes that plagued the plant in Bhopal prior to yesterday's calamity. Here are a few more chilling facts:

☠ Temperature and pressure gauges on the MIC storage unit were so unreliable that workers routinely ignored them.

☠ The refrigeration unit for keeping MIC from over-heating had been shut down for some time.

☠ Last night, the storage tank's alarm failed to notify workers that the tank was overfilled.

☠ A storage tank intended for reserve use in the event of a leak was itself already full of MIC.

THE DAILY ☠ DISASTER

Tuesday, January 28, 1986   Volume CXXXVII No. 28   Price: 25 cents

THE U.S. SPACE SHUTTLE *CHALLENGER* EXPLODES

SEVEN ASTRONAUTS KILLED OVER KENNEDY SPACE CENTER

CAPE CANAVERAL, FLORIDA—Just moments after takeoff today, the space shuttle *Challenger* blew up over Florida, killing all seven astronauts aboard. It is the worst tragedy in the space shuttle program's history.

Challenger lifted off at 11:38 this morning. Just over a minute after leaving the ground, at an altitude of approximately 45,000 feet (13,715 m), flames were seen trailing out of the spacecraft's right solid rocket booster. "Seconds later, the whole thing went up in a ball of smoke and fire," said 26-year-old eyewitness Patricia Torsel. "The giant rocket boosters were blown free of the shuttle—they continued flying wildly about, tracing erratic arcs of smoke in the sky as wreckage from the explosion hurtled toward the ocean." Observers like Torsel, gathered in droves as they always are for shuttle launches, could only stare in stunned silence. "I've certainly never seen anything like this before," she said.

The 25th shuttle mission

The Challenger *space shuttle exploded just one minute after takeoff, killing everyone on board.*

seemed troubled from the very start. The launch had already been postponed four times—twice due to weather. The latest delay occurred yesterday, when ground servicing equipment couldn't be removed from its place alongside the orbiter.

Workers had to saw through the fixture to release it, and by the time they were finished, cross-winds had picked up, exceeding the Kennedy Space Center's safe limits.

This morning broke clear and cold. At the Kennedy Space

IN OTHER NEWS:

THE NEXT STAGE IN TECHNO-FUN

Take a sneak peak at the new electronic game system about to be released by the Japanese corporation Nintendo. See FUN AND GAMES.

DEEP SPACE SPY

The *Voyager 2* probe sends back information about the planet Uranus. See SCIENCE AND TECHNOLOGY.

...AND SPEAKING OF STARS...

Starting this season, Oprah Winfrey is going to have her own show. See ENTERTAINMENT.

Center, *Challenger*'s launch had to wait until the temperature rose above 40° F (4.4° C). Until today, 53° F (11.7° C) had been the record low for a shuttle launch.

The unusually cold weather *(continued on page 2)*

IT'S A SPACESHIP. NO, IT'S AN AIRPLANE. WAIT, IT'S A SPACESHIP. AN AIRPLANE. NO, WAIT...

With Ben Daire, staff travel correspondent

With more than 2.5 million parts, 230 miles (370 km) of wires, and some 1,440 electric circuit breakers, the space shuttle is one of the most sophisticated vehicles ever produced. It stands 122 feet (37 m) long with a wingspan of 78 feet (24 m), has enough cargo space to hold a city bus, and is powered by engines that produce more than a million pounds of thrust. Because it needs to fly both in earth's atmosphere and in outer space, it has to wear a lot of hats. At liftoff, it's a rocket; in orbit, it's a spacecraft; when returning to earth, it's a glider; and when landing, it's an airplane. That's versatility!

The Challenger *crew included teacher Christa McAuliffe, far left.*

★ ★ ★ ★ ★ ★ ★ ★ ★ ★ ★ ★ ★ ★ ★ ★ ★ ★ ★

SHOOTING FOR THE STARS

Learn about these famous space flights in history!

SPUTNIK was the first artificial satellite to be successfully placed in orbit around the earth. It was launched in 1957.

SKYLAB was NASA's first space station, a manned ship that orbited the earth for six years. It was launched in 1973.

APOLLO 11 was the first mission during which humans walked on the surface of the moon. NASA sent Neil Armstrong, Buzz Aldrin, and Michael Collins on this mission, launched in 1969.

VIKING 1 was the first ship to land on Mars and send back photographs of the planet's surface and atmosphere. It was launched in 1975.

★ ★ ★ ★ ★ ★ ★ ★ ★ ★ ★ ★ ★ ★ ★ ★ ★ ★ ★

(continued from page 1)

wasn't the only first. Aboard *Challenger* was Sharon Christa McAuliffe, the first citizen in space. She had outshone 11,000 other applicants from across the United States to become the winner of NASA's Teacher in Space Project. McAuliffe, a social sciences instructor, was scheduled to give a lecture from orbit to students across the country. Unfortunately, it wasn't her lesson that millions of students watched today, but her terrifying demise. Years from now, no doubt, people will recall where they were and what they were doing when Christa McAuliffe and the other six members of *Challenger*'s crew lost their lives to tragedy.

"O" NO!

With Moe Mentum, staff physicist

The space shuttle gets most of its lift during liftoff from two rocket boosters, towering thrusters attached to the ship's flanks that allow it to speed faster than sound into the highest reaches of the atmosphere (together, the two solid-fuel rocket boosters produce thrust that's equivalent to 32 747 jumbo jets). There, before entering space, they are detached and allowed to fall back to earth, where they splash harmlessly into the ocean. When these boosters fire, the incredible heat and pressure makes them expand, requiring something to fill in the gaps between the booster's sections so that burning fuel doesn't escape. That "something" is an O-ring, a thin circle of synthetic material that's tough enough—and flexible enough—to hold back the force of the blasting rockets. It is possible that this morning's frigid temperatures made the O-rings brittle, preventing them from expanding properly during the flight. That's where the initial flames came from: they were leaking past a faulty O-ring. Further investigation by on-site scientists will be looking into this possibility. We will update this story as more concrete information becomes available.

THE DAILY ☠ DISASTER

Tuesday, April 29, 1986 | Volume CXXXVI No. 119 | Price: 25 cents

Meltdown: Nuclear Nightmare Comes True in Soviet Union

RADIATION FALLOUT LEAKS FROM RUPTURED FACILITY IN CHERNOBYL

CHERNOBYL, UKRAINE—There is a new word in the vocabulary of fear: Chernobyl. Three days ago, at a nuclear power plant near there, the unthinkable finally happened—a meltdown occurred, releasing massive amounts of radioactive contaminants into the atmosphere. It is the worst nuclear accident in history.

Evidence of the disaster was first discovered in the West by scientists in Sweden, who detected levels of radiation in the air and grass that were much higher than normal. Soon it was obvious to scientists all over Scandinavia that some sort of core meltdown had occurred in the Ukraine region of the Soviet Union. Only now are Russian officials admitting publicly to the accident (thanks for the heads-up, fellas).

It all began harmlessly enough when, early on the 25th, the plant crew decided to conduct a test. In the event of a loss of main electrical power to the plant, diesel generators are on hand to provide power. However, it takes them 50 sec-

A nuclear meltdown occurred at the Chernobyl Power Plant in the Ukraine three days ago—and Russian officials are only now reporting it.

onds to reach full strength. "The test was to see how long the turbines in the reactor would continue running without full power during that 50-second period while the diesel generators came online," said 25-year-old plant employee Vladimir Shostokovich. "It was an ideal time for such a test, as Unit 4 was scheduled to be shut down for maintenance anyway."

The test was then postponed by the grid controller in Kiev, who insisted that the reactor needed to be kept at normal operating levels to provide electricity. The actual test was conducted after 1:00 A.M. that morning. Twenty minutes into the test, an increase in steam within the core sent the reactor into an uncontrollable power surge. Four minutes later, internal pressures reached 120 times

IN OTHER NEWS

"MARCIA, MARCIA, MARCIA!"
Celebrating her birthday today is Eve Plumb, the actress who played Jan on *The Brady Bunch*. Find out where she is today. See ENTERTAINMENT.

THE ROCKET
Boston Red Sox pitcher Roger Clemens struck out 20 batters today in a game against the Seattle Mariners. See SPORTS.

LITERARY LOSS
More than 800,000 books were destroyed today when a fire engulfed the Los Angeles Central Library. See CURRENT EVENTS.

the normal power, resulting in two explosions that allowed air into the inflammable interior, causing a reactor fire. "Suddenly, the core spewed out a wave of toxic materials," recalled Shostokovich, "including eight tons (8.8 metric tons) of fuel (which consists of plutonium), a portion of the radioactive graphite blocks, and cesium and iodine *(continued on page 2)*

(continued on page 2)

(continued from page 1)

vapors—all of which are about as healthy for you as the atmosphere of Venus." Thirty-one people were killed in the plant—all but two of these deaths resulted from exposure to radiation.

"As you might imagine, our medical staff instantly became the most popular people in the plant," another employee, 49-year-old Konstantin Aromiov commented, "but to no avail. The on-site nurse station was empty, and some of its facilities were locked up for the night."

The twin explosions have created some 30 fires throughout the plant. Despite the efforts of firefighters from all over the area, many of those fires continue to burn today. But the worst is clearly yet to come: All over Scandinavia and Eastern Europe, high radioactive levels are being detected. Who knows how far the wind will carry the dangerous fallout?

FIZZLIN' FISSION!
With Moe Mentum, staff physicist

Nuclear reactors provide power by splitting atoms, a process called *fission*. It's the same principle behind the atom bombs—only at nuclear reactors, the power is harnessed for energy, not for killing people. The Soviet design of the Chernobyl reactor produces an effect called *positive void coefficient,* which basically means that an excess of steam creates an increase in power that can spiral out of control. Other reactors around the world have positive void coefficients, but they are built with mechanisms that control it. Soviet reactors, on the other hand, lack these controlling measures, which allow them to become unstable when operating at low power levels.

HEROES OF THE WEEK

Immediately after the terrible fires broke out at the Chernobyl plant, Lieutenant Pravik, commander of the Chernobyl fire crew, alerted fire departments all over the Kiev region. As soon as they arrived, they set about their extremely dangerous duty with heroic speed and effort. Their job was made tougher by the fact that no fire drill had ever been conducted at the plant. Worse, while those who battle nuclear fires in other nations have specially designed protective clothing to wear, none of the firemen at the Chernobyl blaze were so equipped. As they fought the flames at close range within the reactor building, they willingly exposed themselves to lethal doses of radiation. Their valiant struggle helped contain the disaster, but at a terrible price: many of them died from radiation sickness.

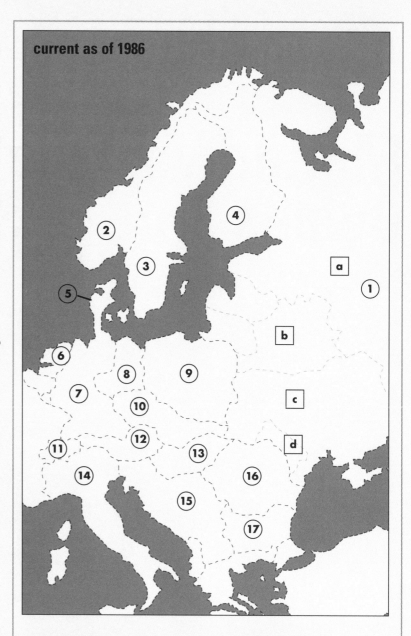

current as of 1986

WHO'S AT RISK?

Although there's no telling how far the wind may carry the nuclear fallout from Chernobyl (it could reach Asia and North America), those nations closest to the disaster are at greatest risk from the radiation.

Can you name the countries numbered in this map of Europe?

Answers

1. USSR
2. Norway
3. Sweden
4. Finland
5. Denmark
6. Netherlands
7. West Germany
8. East Germany
9. Poland
10. Czechoslovakia
11. Switzerland
12. Austria
13. Hungary
14. Italy
15. Yugoslavia
16. Romania
17. Bulgaria

a. Russia
b. Belarus
c. Ukraine
d. Moldava

THE DAILY ☠ DISASTER

Friday, March 24, 1989   Volume CXXXIXI No. 83   Price: 25 cents

Oil Tanker Makes Slick Move Near Valdez, Alaska

WORST OIL SPILL EVER IN U.S. WATERS

WHAT'S AT STAKE?

Prince William Sound is a pristine environment. Grizzly bears, countless varieties of birds, otters, and a wide range of marine life all make it their home. The area also supports a large fishing community, upon whose success the local economy depends. Oil, with its capacity to pollute beaches, coat and kill animals, and poison fish, may very well destroy the sound's delicate balance. Only time will tell how thorough the damage is.

VALDEZ, ALASKA—Just after midnight this morning, the oil tanker *Exxon Valdez* ran aground in Prince William Sound, just 25 miles (40 km) from the Alaskan town for which it was named. As much as 250,000 barrels (10.5 million gallons, or 40 million L) of crude oil have escaped the tanker's ruptured hull, making it the worst oil spill ever to have occurred in U.S. waters. It is every environmentalist's worst nightmare.

The tanker departed the Alyeska Marine Terminal last night around 9:30 P.M. after taking on its cargo of crude oil. It then made its way south through the Valdez Arm, a body of water that opens onto Prince William Sound, and through which all tankers going to and from Valdez must pass. Shortly after 11:30 P.M., the vessel headed out of the usual shipping lane to avoid oncoming ice. This was a risky move, for ships must remain within the lanes to avoid the small islands that dot these waters. Right around midnight, the third mate—who, while the

The cleanup of Prince William Sound, Alaska, is going to be a long, hard job.

master was off the bridge, was in command of the ship—phoned the master and said, "I think we're in big trouble."

He had a gift for understatement. As soon as he hung up the phone, *Exxon Valdez* shuddered ominously. It had struck ground on Bligh Reef. The crew then tried maneuvering the ship off its sandy snag, but to no avail. By noon today, the foundered ship had belched out an oil slick three miles wide by five miles long (4.8 x 8 km), placing the precious ecosystem of Prince William Sound in dire jeopardy.

"We're already investigating how the crew let this happen," said investigator Martin Krueger.

"For one thing, the master of the ship, Joseph Hazelwood, had complete confidence in his third mate, Gregory Cousins, despite the fact that Cousins was suffering from exhaustion due to excessive workload, and should not have been put in such a position at that time. Also, why hadn't the ship's navigational watch spotted the oncoming reef?"

Another suspicious piece of evidence has turned up: it seems that Hazelwood was reportedly not paying very close attention to the course of his ship. That's little comfort for all the volunteers and organizations that have arrived on the scene to help clean up his mess!

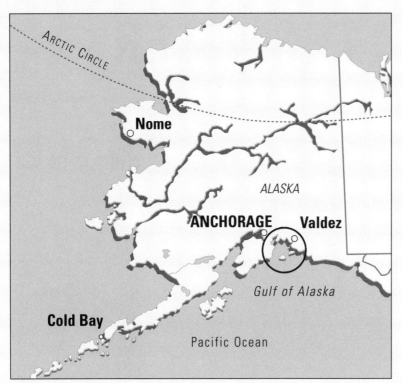

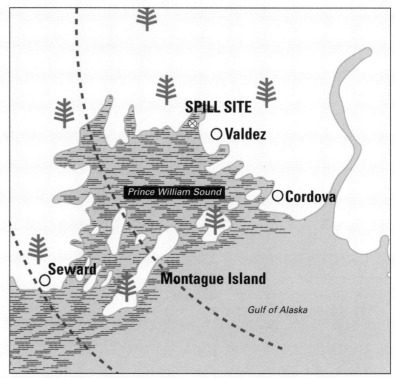

Prince William Sound, located near Valdez, Alaska, is now an oily mess, thanks to the Exxon Valdez's *crash. The lines on the map at right show the oil's progression southwest as shifting tides distributed the oil farther and farther along the coast.*

NOT YOUR AVERAGE MESS
With Autumn Greenacre, staff ecologist

Response to the spill has been slow and disorganized. (In fact, local fisherman from the town of Cordova offered to help the Coast Guard in the cleanup, only to be turned down.) This is a pity, as the oil spreads farther with every moment. And getting 250,000 barrels of oil out of the ocean is no picnic—here are some options:

● **Boom:** The backbone of every oil spill cleanup, this involves dragging a special absorbent chain across the surface, soaking up and gathering oil as it moves.

● **Burning:** Torching the stuff leaves a residue that is easily scooped out of the water; it also produces a giant cloud of nasty black smoke that does a real number on the atmosphere.

● **Dispersants:** These chemicals can break up the oil and spread it around, making it less concentrated. Unfortunately, they don't actually take the oil out of the water.

● **Skimming:** Because oil is lighter than water, it floats, allowing it to be picked up by specially designed ships called *skimmers.*

● **Bioremediation:** Believe it or not, there are actually microbes that devour oil (they're not very smart—but then, most microbes aren't). Bioremediation is a process whereby special fertilizers are used to increase the number of these microbes.

● **Hot water washing:** Hot water makes the oil less sticky and it can be more easily skimmed off.

CLEAN UP YOUR ACT
With Professor Cornelius III

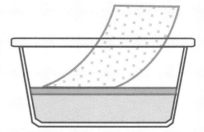

Here's an activity that will give you an idea of just what these guys are up against.

What You Need:

Large bowl

Water

Vegetable oil

Wire strainer

Paper towel

Spoon

Simulate the Spill:

1. Fill a large bowl or dishpan with cold water.

2. Pour half a cup of vegetable oil into the water.

   You'll notice that it rises right to the top (the water is heavier, forcing the oil to rise).

3. Try to skim the oil off the top of the water using a wire skimmer.

4. Try to skim the oil using a paper towel.

5. Try skimming with a spoon. See how much oil you were able to remove? It's hard work, isn't it?

THE DAILY DISASTER

Tuesday, August 25. 1992   Volume CXLII No. 238   Price: 25 cents

Andrew Takes Southern Florida for a Spin

HORRIBLE HURRICANE MOST EXPENSIVE DISASTER IN U.S. HISTORY

DADE COUNTY, FLORIDA— There's a name that not many new parents in this part of the country are likely to christen their sons in the near future, and it starts with "A." Announcing the start of the hurricane season with a deafening roar, Hurricane Andrew slammed into southern Florida yesterday, causing unprecedented damage.

After whipping through the Bahamas, Andrew stormed across the Florida Straits, making landfall early yesterday morning. Residents in the heavily populated region south of downtown Miami began their day by witnessing what a Category 4 hurricane can do when it really hits its stride (Category 5 is the strongest). Winds blew as high as 164 mph (264 km/h). Whole communities were wiped out in what many are already calling one of the worst natural disasters in American history.

The results of the hurricane's wrath are staggering: In the four hours it took for Andrew to blast its way across the southern tip of Florida, well over 70,000 homes were destroyed, leaving some 200,000 people homeless. Around 600,000 homes and businesses have lost electrical and phone service, affecting 1.4 million people, and water and sewerage facilities are a complete shambles.

Widespread looting has already begun, as police and emergency personnel try to cope with a road and communications system that has collapsed. "You've got to keep your eye out for thieves," said 35-year-old survivor Bob

Cars spun into the air and out of control in the deadly hurricane that hit Florida's coast.

Carrol. "I don't have much left after the storm, but you can bet your buttons I'm not letting someone else just walk off with it." The death toll is estimated at around 40—a figure that, given the severity of the damage, is incredibly low.

But it is the economic devastation that has ensured Andrew's place in the Hurricane Hall of Fame. Estimates are likely to exceed a whopping $20 billion, making Andrew the single costliest disaster in the nation's history.

Hardest hit was the little community of Homestead. "Our town has virtually ceased to exist," said 69-year-old local Jim Alenby. "There used to be row upon row of mobile homes. Now they're all gone. Nothing but piles of rubbish left." Although authorities issued warnings to evacuate, only 65% of residents chose to comply.

Experts here had been keeping a wary eye on Andrew's course since it first became a tropical storm on August 17. By the 22nd, the system had graduated to hurricane status, crossing the Bahamas late on the 23rd and into the 24th, when it headed for the mainland.

The worst part? Andrew seems ready for more. It appears to be gaining strength over the Gulf of Mexico, and heading in a northerly direction. Louisiana, look out.

IS IT A BOY OR A GIRL?

With Professor Cornelius IV

Hurricanes are named by the National Hurricane Center when they're still in the tropical storm stage. It's a tradition that started in 1950. In 1953, female names were used for the first time, and the practice of alternating between male and female names began in 1979. Each list of names is reused every six years, except those that cause a great deal of destruction (like our boy Andrew here); those names are retired, kind of like the jerseys of celebrated sports stars.

STANDING GUARD

On average, 10 tropical storms develop each year over the Atlantic Ocean, Caribbean Sea, and Gulf of Mexico. Of those, six or so are bound to become hurricanes. So who's keeping an eye on them? The folks at the National Hurricane Center, that's who. They're located near Miami, Florida—close to the action. After they've spotted a hurricane that looks like it might be heading for land, they start watching it like a hawk, trying to predict where it will drift. (Computers have made their job a lot easier in recent decades.) If they issue a hurricane watch, it means that hurricane conditions could hit land within 24 to 36 hours (you can kiss your beach party good-bye). When they issue a hurricane warning, hold on to your hat—hurricane conditions could be here in less than a day. Predictions like these allow local authorities to prepare emergency services and help you get the heck out of town. Just ask the citizens of southern Florida— you don't want to be around when a hurricane pays a visit.

HURRICANE: GREAT WHITE PINWHEEL OF DESTRUCTION

With Harry Kane, Jr., staff meteorologist

Hurricanes spiral like giant pinwheels that measure several hundred miles in diameter. At the center is the eye of the hurricane, which is calm and usually measures about 20 miles (32 km) in diameter. The wall of clouds that surround the eye is where the hurricane's ferocious winds and thunderstorms occur, spinning out from the center in gigantic arms of very nasty weather. It all gets started over tropical oceans, where water vapor is pushed upward by warm seas and turned into thunderstorms. Add the right combination of heat, moisture, and wind conditions, and those thunderstorms will get together and form a "tropical depression," featuring winds of 38 mph (61 km/h) or less. If the system keeps building, it will turn into a "tropical storm," with winds of 39 to 73 mph (63 to 117 km/h). Once the winds are 74 mph (119 km/h) or worse, you've got a hurricane. Because they draw their power from warm water, hurricanes are capable of lasting much longer at sea than over land. Unfortunately, that fact doesn't stop some of them from heading for shore, where they end up causing so much trouble and damage.

GETTING THE DROP ON HURRICANE SEASON

With Captain Caution, staff safety consultant

If you live near the Gulf of Mexico or on the Atlantic Coast, you should make sure your family prepares your home for hurricanes before they strike. Windows should be covered with plywood—half-inch marine plywood is ideal. Also, make sure to trim any weak or dead tree branches that are nearby—hurricane winds can turn them into projectiles. Here are some other things to keep in mind:

- Plan an evacuation route— your local Red Cross chapter can tell you what the community hurricane preparedness plan is.

- Have disaster supplies on hand, such as flashlights, portable radios, first aid kit, canned food, manual can opener, cash, credit cards, and sturdy shoes.

- Ask an out-of-state friend or relative to serve as the family contact (after a disaster, it's often easier to call long distance than local).

- Last but not least, make arrangements for your pets— because animals are not allowed in emergency shelters, you'll have to place Fido or Spot in the local animal shelter.

THE DAILY DISASTER

Monday, March 15, 1993   Volume CXLIII No. 74   Price: 25 cents

"Storm of the Century" Puts A Full Nelson on East Coast

EVERY MAJOR EASTERN AIRPORT CLOSED

NEW YORK, NEW YORK— There are storms, and there are Storms. This one truly takes the cake. From the Gulf of Mexico to eastern Canada, the weather has gone completely berserk for three days. Tornadoes, blizzards, hurricane-force winds—you name it, this storm's got it. For the first time ever, all major airports in the eastern third of the United States have closed. This really is the Storm of the Century.

As early as the beginning of this month, weather forecasters all over North America were gaping in awe at the storm that was brewing. A huge mass of cold air was moving down from the North Pole. The real trouble started when it ran into a warmer body of air over the Gulf of Mexico. Violent thunderstorms started forming all along the front between these two air masses, and the whole mess gradually evolved into a single, giant, spinning storm system. Warnings went out,

A resident attempts to dig her car out of more than three feet of snow in Larchmont, New York.

but people all over the country were still caught unprepared.

The monstrous winter storm struck land on the morning of March 12, whaling on Florida with high winds and storm surges that sent ocean water flooding into the coast. "Holy Cow!" said 26-year-old homeowner Nathan Gazebo, just one of countless Floridians to have his world turned upside down. "My house was blitzed by 20-foot (6-m) waves. What the water

didn't take away, the wind smashed to pieces." Even tornadoes got into the act: an estimated 15 of them touched down, killing 44 people. The storm then started making its way up the East Coast, buffeting everything in its path with hurricane-force winds.

As it moved north, the rain turned to snow—lots of snow. Covering a staggering 2,000 miles (3,200 km), it dumped a foot (30 cm) of the white stuff *(continued on page 2)*

(continued on page 2)

IN OTHER NEWS

WHERE EVERYBODY KNOWS YOUR NAME

After a popular 10-year run, the hit show *Cheers* is entering its final season. See ENTERTAINMENT.

THE LAW ACCORDING TO JANET

Read our interview with recently appointed U.S. Attorney General Janet Reno, the first woman to hold that office. See POLITICS.

FOR THE BIRDS

What do hockey fans think of the NHL's newest expansion team, Disney's Mighty Ducks? See SPORTS.

AS UNIQUE AS A SNOWFLAKE!

Snowflakes form when the water falling from a cloud freezes—but it's not so simple! A single drop of water may fall through some really cold air and freeze, then hit some warm air and start to melt, only to freeze up again. All this freezing and refreezing—and sometimes freezing at different temperatures—can cause strange effects in a snowflake's pattern. Also, there are bits of dust in the air that come into contact with the droplet and can affect a snowflake's pattern too. Because no two snowflakes encounter exactly the same dust particles, or temperature shifts, in exactly the same way, no two snowflakes end up looking exactly the same!

(continued on page 2)
on virtually every stretch of land between Alabama and Maine. Some areas received more than 40 inches (100 cm). Byron McEnzie, a 37-year-old resident of Winston-Salem, North Carolina, was one of those caught unprepared. "Snow? In North Carolina? And this much of it? I don't know, I just don't know. We don't have enough snowplows to handle it." Even farther north, piles and piles of snow arrived. Interstate highways have been closed, and millions of people have lost electrical power. An estimated 25% of the nation's airline flights have been cancelled.

An estimated 250 people have already died, and the damage nationwide is sure to run into the billions of dollars. As if all that weren't enough, temperatures throughout the East remain at record lows—in other words, the snow isn't going anywhere anytime soon.

WHY IS SNOW WHITE?
With Moe Mentum, staff physicist

Sunlight is composed of the visible spectrum: the colors violet, blue, green, yellow, orange, and red. The specific color of something is determined by which colors in the visible spectrum it reflects. Snow crystals, which are made of tiny little angles, reflect every part of the spectrum. Therefore, they're without color—in other words, white.

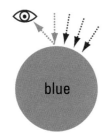
blue

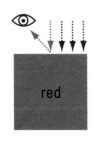
red

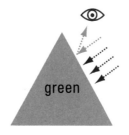
green

BE IN THE KNOW WHEN IT COMES TO SNOW
With Harry Kane, Jr., staff meteorologist

The Storm of the Century has plastered huge areas of the country with snow, many of which have never even seen the stuff before. Seeing as it's likely to be around for a while, we all might as well get comfortable with it. See how much you know about the subject with this *Daily Disaster* quiz:

True or False?

Sometimes it's actually too cold to snow.

🌡 **Answer:** False. As long as there is some moisture in the air and some way to lift it (and thereby cool it), it can snow even at incredibly low temperatures.

Snowflakes can be as big as 2 inches (5 cm) across.

🌡 **Answer:** True. Flakes of that size have been measured, usually in conditions that feature near-freezing temperatures and light winds.

Snow can help keep you warm.

🌡 **Answer:** True! Because of the shape of individual crystals, snow traps a lot of air—fresh drifts of snow are typically 95% air. That means it makes a good insulator; if you were to bury yourself in fresh snow, your body heat would be less likely to escape than if you were out in the open (just make sure you leave a hole for breathing!).

The colder the temperature outside, the easier it is to make good snowballs.

🌡 **Answer:** False. The closer the snow's temperature is to melting point (around 32–25° F, or 0–4° degrees C), the more likely the snow is to be sticky (ideal for good snowballs). The farther away the snow's temperature gets from melting point, the harder it gets, until eventually it's like sand (just try making a snowman out of that!).

THE DAILY DISASTER

Friday, July 16, 1993   Volume CXLIII No. 197   Price: 25 cents

Killer Bees Claim Their First Victim in the United States

DEADLY NEW NEIGHBORS NOT JUST PASSING THROUGH, ARE HERE TO STAY

HARLINGEN, TEXAS—Americans now have firsthand experience of how killer bees got their name. Yesterday, 82-year-old Lino Lopez became the first person in the United States to die from being stung by the deadly insects.

"Lopez was attempting to remove a colony of bees from an abandoned building on his ranch," said police investigator Dudley Dobbs. "Well, that turned out to be a real bad idea." The bees objected to being disturbed and proceeded to display the deadly behavior for which they have earned a reputation throughout Central and South America. "Lopez was stung more than 40 times," said Dobbs. Though nearly 200 people have been attacked since the little devils first appeared north of Mexico, this is the first fatality.

Killer bees are referred to by experts as *Africanized* bees because of their origin. During the 1950s, scientists in Brazil tried to create a bee with enhanced honey-producing

Scientist study killer bee behavior in the laboratory.

qualities. They brought queen bees over from southern Africa and began breeding them with local specimens. Unfortunately, African bees are much more aggressive than their South American counterparts. In 1957, 26 of those African queens escaped from the experimental apiary (a place where bees are bred). They proceeded to mate with local bee populations, creating colonies of so-called Africanized bees that exhibited the same deadly behavior. Their numbers rapidly grew, spreading into most of South America. Since 1957 they have been steadily spreading northward at a rate of around 200 miles (over 320 km) per year, moving up through Central America.

By 1990 they had made it to the United States, where they were first spotted near Hidalgo, Texas. "Africanized bees are 10 times as likely to react violently to intruders than are regular honey bees," said insect expert Mary Ann Handlan. "Sometimes just standing near a colony is enough to get them riled." They don't even like the vibrations from nearby car engines. Moreover, they will typically chase their victims for very long distances.

There's more bad news. Because Africanized bees look *(continued on page 2)*

(continued from page 1)
virtually identical to regular bees, they're impossible to recognize by sight alone (even experts usually have to put one under a microscope to get a positive identification). And, although their sting is slightly less powerful, they're far more likely to swarm—in other words, a lot more of them will drop everything and go on the attack.

As of yet, no effective means of halting their progress has been found—which means that at least a few more folks are likely to meet the same fate as poor Lino Lopez. Hundreds of people have been stung to death in South America alone.

So how far north are they likely to get? Opinion is divided: some insist that only the southern and southwestern states will be affected, while others think that they could take hold much farther north, perhaps as far as the Canadian border.

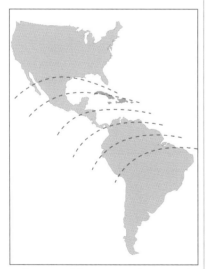

Africanized bees are making steady progress northward.

BEE CAREFUL!
With Rose Greenacre, staff ecologist

Africanized bees are less choosy about where they nest. They'll even take up residence in overturned flower pots, utility boxes, or holes in the ground. It's best, therefore, to keep an eye out for them and stay far away from their homes. Here are some other useful facts:

🐝 Bees tend to attack dark things, so wear light colored clothing.

🐝 Make it difficult for them to nest near your home by filling holes in the ground, caulking cracks in walls, and getting rid of garbage quickly (they love the smell, and will gladly turn a soda can into a hive).

🐝 Look for bees that are acting strangely—they'll often exhibit defensive behavior before going on the attack.

🐝 Should you find bees, stay away and call a pest control company.

🐝 If you're attacked, seek shelter in an enclosed place (like a house or car), and don't jump in water—the bees will just hover above waiting for you to surface.

🐝 When stung, remove the stinger as soon as possible—it will continue to pump venom even after the bee dies (all bees die after they sting); the best way is to slide it out sideways with a hard, flat surface.

THE BUZZ ON THE BUZZ
With Professor Cornelius IV

All bees, whether Africanized or not, are divided up into three different types: queens, workers, and drones. In addition to the queen, there are workers who fly around extracting pollen from flowers, and drones who mate with the queen. Honeybees are vital to American agriculture: not only do they produce $150 million worth of honey each year, but they're also used to help produce over 90 different crops. They do this by carrying pollen from plant to plant, helping the crops grow and thrive. Test your knowledge of bees with the *Daily Disaster* Bzzz Quiz:

1. A typical small hive will contain:
   a. 5,000 bees
   b. 10,000 bees
   c. 20,000 bees
   d. 100,000 bees

2. The primary responsibility of the queen is to:
   a. Sit around and eat
   b. Protect the hive
   c. Build a throne of wax
   d. Lay eggs

3. The worker bees construct the hive's honeycomb out of:
   a. Wax
   b. Concrete
   c. Wood chips
   d. Pollen

4. Which of the following are bees most closely related to?
   a. Spiders
   b. Butterflies
   c. Ants
   d. Beetles

Answers: 1) c, 2) d, 3) a, 4) c.

TASTE THE NECTAR!

Bees produce honey, a wonderful, sweet food that never spoils! You can cook with it, too. Make these honey cookies with an adult!

Ingredients:

3 eggs

2 cups honey

½ cup milk

2 teaspoons baking soda

4½ cups all-purpose flour

Directions:

1. Preheat the oven to 350° F (175° C).

2. In a medium bowl, beat the eggs well. Add honey, milk, and baking soda and beat until combined.

3. Mix in the flour until just combined.

4. Drop by spoonfuls onto an ungreased baking sheet, spaced approximately 2 inches (5 cm) apart.

5. Bake for 8 to 10 minutes, or until golden brown.

6. Let cool on a cooling rack, and serve!

THE DAILY DISASTER

Monday, August 2, 1993   Volume CXLIII No. 214   Price: 25 cents

Mississippi Does It Again

WORST FLOOD IN AMERICAN HISTORY RAVAGES MIDWEST

ST. LOUIS, MISSOURI—In St. Louis, the Mississippi River has been above flood stage since April 1. Today, the river reached a crest of 49 feet, 7 inches (15 m)—which means enough water is flowing past this point on the river to fill Busch Stadium every 65 seconds (that would make for some wet baseballs!). The climax of a flood that started in June has turned much of the Midwest into a giant swimming pool. An estimated 793 billion gallons (3 billion cu. m) of water have saturated the floodplain downriver from St. Louis.

Ironically, the National Weather Service had predicted back in March that this summer would see lower than average rainfall. They couldn't have been further off the mark, as these past five months have shown.

On June 10, severe storms started covering large areas of Wisconsin, Minnesota, and the Dakotas with eight inches (20 cm) of rain. Ten days after the rainstorms began, a dam on the Black River in

The entire Midwest is covered in water—every major tributary of the Mississippi River has spilled its banks.

Wisconsin broke—it would be the first of many throughout the Mississippi River system. On the same day, the upper 200 miles (322 km) of the Mississippi River were closed to boats or other river traffic. By July 10, Fort Madison, Iowa, had alone experienced rain for 54 of the previous 58 days.

"By July 15th, a huge area covering parts of nine states—North Dakota, South Dakota, Nebraska, Kansas, Missouri, Iowa, Wisconsin, Minnesota, and Illinois—had received twice its normal rainfall," said St. Louis meteorologist Stanley Wake. "Such torrential down-

pours can force even the largest rivers to overflow their banks. Every major tributary of the Mississippi has been affected, including the Missouri, Kansas, Illinois, Des Moines, and Wisconsin Rivers."

But rain is only part of the problem. Because of the cooler temperatures this area experienced last year, less water evaporated, making the ground more saturated even before the rains began. This means that more water ran into the rivers and streams, and then flooded the land, instead of being absorbed by the earth.

Wetlands along the Mississippi and its tributaries

IN OTHER NEWS

GOING, GOING, GONE!

Baseball slugger Reggie Jackson voted into the Hall of Fame in Cooperstown, New York. See SPORTS.

FULL OF BEANS

Strange little critters called "Beanie Babies" are turning up in toy stores around the country. See TRENDS.

I SCREAM, YOU SCREAM, WE ALL SCREAM . . .

Sweet tooths from coast to coast cool off with a favorite treat on official Ice Cream Sandwich Day. See YUM YUM.

normally act as safety valves for flooding—they take on overflow, acting as natural reservoirs for floodwaters. But as much as 80% of the original wetlands in this region have been drained since the 1940s to make room for communities and agricultural land. Therefore, the water has nowhere to go—except onto *(continued on page 2)*

OUR READERS RESPOND

Nancy Klufine, 48, real estate agent

"My parents were in the great flood of 1927. I live on the outskirts of St. Louis, and now I understand what they went through. I wish my parents would consider moving somewhere far, far away from the Mississippi River. It's just too unpredictable."

Bud Overling, 39, fireman:

"The Mississippi is one of the greatest river systems in the world, and an extremely powerful force of nature. We've got to stop building along its banks and trying to control it with levees. No matter how prepared we think we are, the river always proves us wrong. It's just too big to try to control."

Ray Kozlowski, 69, butcher:

"How can something like this happen in the richest country on earth? Haven't we learned enough to be able to prepare for this? It seems we haven't put enough time or resources into making sure people are safe and property is protected. It's amazing how much damage water can do."

(continued from page 1)

the unfortunate people who live nearby. The houses built over drained wetlands are the first to feel the effects of a heavy rainfall. The death toll could climb as high as 50.

The damage caused has been catastrophic: some 150 levees (the man-made walls that contain the rivers at their banks) have failed, $12 billion in property damage has been done, 16,000 square miles (41,000 sq. km) of farmland are under water, and a total of 17 million acres (7 million hectares) have been flooded. Countless thousands of people have been made homeless, and the economic impact from ruined crops is likely to be crippling.

IT'S IN THE BAG

Sandbags have been a vital part of resistance to the floodwaters. If you stack them fast enough, high enough, and in the right places, you can protect property that would otherwise find itself underwater. More than 26 million of them have been used since the floods began back in June (mostly by individual homeowners, who have to fill their own). That means that more than 925 million pounds (420 million kg) of fill have been stuffed into bags.

BE PREPARED!

With Captain Caution, staff safety consultant

Here's an activity that could save someone's life—possibly yours. Assemble an emergency supplies kit that contains:

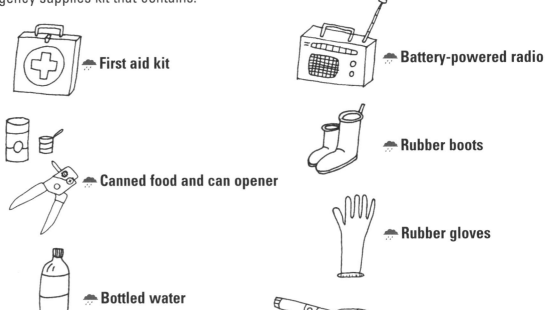

- First aid kit
- Battery-powered radio
- Canned food and can opener
- Rubber boots
- Rubber gloves
- Bottled water
- Flashlight and extra batteries

THE DAILY DISASTER

Sunday, December 19, 1999   Volume CXLIX No. 353   Price: 25 cents

A Mudslide Deluge Buries Thousands in Venezuela

TORRENTIAL DOWNPOUR SENDS EARTH SLIP-SLIDING AWAY

CARACAS, VENEZUELA—It is not only Venezuela's worst natural disaster in half a century, but probably its dirtiest. Ten days of heavy rain have flooded much of the northern part of the country, creating mudslides that carried away whole communities. More than 5,000 have surely died, and the fatalities may rise to as many as 10,000.

More than 75% of Venezuela's population is in the northern part of the country, where rain continues to fall in sheets. One hundred people are feared dead in the capital, Caracas, where flash floods have turned alleys into streams and streets into rivers.

But the worst damage has occurred in the shantytowns that occupy the sides of mountains. Here, the rain-saturated ground created mudslides that went crashing down steep inclines, carrying away whole communities. Blandin, a hillside village that sits on a mountain north of Caracas, was demolished by an avalanche of mud. Flimsy shacks construct-

Cars, homes, and people have been covered in mud since the horrible mudslides began ten days ago.

ed of brick and tin don't last long when the ground starts moving. In the valleys below, huge piles of mud and boulders cover cars, homes, fences, yards. "Everywhere are heaps of debris captured in brown prisons," says Emilio Consuela, a 29-year-old police officer. "Many victims are trying to salvage what they can from the mud, but nearly everything is buried too deeply."

More than 80,000 troops have been mobilized to aid in rescue operations. They must

also maintain control of stricken areas—looting has already occurred in some areas. Helicopters can be seen lifting the wounded to safety and carrying in desperately needed supplies. The numbers of homeless are unimaginable: thousands of shocked refugees make their way to camps to find food and shelter. Many, unable to reach transportation by boat or helicopter, are making their way south by foot. Relief efforts are difficult— most of the roads are complete-

ly washed out, making ground transportation impossible.

"It will be quite some time before we know just how many people have been killed," says Dr. Victor Vargas, a relief worker. "So many have been buried beneath the mud. Everywhere, the mud. There are victims we are simply never going to find."

Hugo Chavez, President of Venezuela, was a paratrooper in the army before he got into politics. He has once again donned his uniform to personally lead one of the many army units that are going into disaster areas to aid the injured and homeless and to stop looters. He has appealed to all Venezuelans not affected by the floods and mudslides to take homeless refugees into their homes. His wife, First Lady Marisabel Chavez, has opened the presidential palace to children whose parents are dead or missing. Their example should inspire many Venezuelans during the country's worst natural disaster ever.

HOW TO AVOID SLIPPING UP WHEN IT COMES TO MUDSLIDES

With Captain Caution, staff safety consultant

The best way to avoid mudslides is to not live in a house that's on a slope. Of course, not everyone has that choice. Here's what people whose homes might be in danger can do:

- **Because mudslides (and landslides) are much more likely to occur on slopes without trees and brush, make sure your property—and the property above you—is planted with vegetation. Ground cover is the key.**

- **Another option is to cover the bare slopes with netting made from steel, bundled wire rings, or rope. Such a barrier can keep fine-grained material from getting loose and heading your way down the slope.**

Here are some warning signs that a land- or mudslide may occur, especially after a heavy rain:

- **New cracks in the ground or sidewalk**

- **Decks or patios tilting away from the house**

- **Tilting of floors or foundations**

- **Broken water lines**

- **Leaning telephone or power lines**

- **Sunken roads**

- **Sticking doors**

- **Water levels in creeks that have suddenly changed**

Mudslides: A Slippery Slope

WITH ROSE GREENACRE, STAFF ECOLOGIST

Thousands of people around the world die every year from mudslides. A mudslide is like a landslide, except that the earth is saturated with water when it happens. It all begins when steep slopes on hills or mountains are weakened. Many things can do this: erosion from streams or rivers, heavy rain or lots of melting snow, earthquakes, even vibrations from traffic or construction. Slopes without vegetation are particularly vulnerable, because plants anchor the soil with their roots and prevent the ground from moving easily. Once the slope is weakened, all it needs is a lot of water to set it off—here, they got a torrential downpour. Once the amount of water is too great, gravity does the rest. The mud shifts, sliding downhill, and takes everything with it: rocks, trees, buildings, whatever. They can pick up tremendous speed, becoming tidal waves of mud, wiping out and burying everything in their path.